MW01517690

"This boo
combat and the
survive. Brent tells a powerful story of the
despair, of destruction and healing, with poignancy
and wit that will bring you to tears and laughter. His is
an amazing account of finding wisdom, inspiration and
sanity in a Vietnamese village while all around him the
violence of war brings horror to one and all. We owe
him a debt of thanks for the honest, gut-sharing of his
wounds, his pain, and his search for recovery which
offers hope to all who suffer from PTSD and those
who suffer with them. Dr. Tom Pinkson "

Dr. Tom Pinkson, Psychotherapist

"I ordered this book in an attempt to gain a
deeper understanding of what my dear husband went
through in Vietnam. My need was a personal one,
which this book fulfilled. The journey this veteran took
was long road to understanding his self through being
involved with war veterans the world over. What I
learned was that war leaves horrific scars, physical and
emotional on everyone who has served. It is a book
that had me laughing, crying, hating governments for
beginning wars, and loving the men and women who
serve for their heroism and strength. I highly
recommend this to anyone who has a veteran home
from the Middle East Wars of today or yesterday's
Vietnam War. "

Francis Garneau, Wife of VN Veteran

"This book evokes a visceral response from the reader. It does not assume to sway the reader's opinion on war, but rather educates him/her to the effects of war on soldiers, friends, family and society at large. The author has managed to factually document the results of post-traumatic stress syndrome across the globe. It is a cross-cultural examination which unifies rather than separates. The story itself flows easily and the author has a gift for leading the reader into experiencing foreign sights, sounds, and smells. This true tale is exciting and it is sad. It is gut-wrenching and it is ecstatic. It covers the gamut of human emotion and tells the story of one man who ends up, "Winning the War Within". This is a must read! "

Maria O'Toole, Wife of VN Vet

"If you're looking for a genuine account of the "in country" Vietnam War on the ground, this is a must read. The Author is a Marine Interpreter during combat in the heart of VC strongholds. He captures the surreal nature of war which is at once bizarre, yet based on strategy, psychology, deception and chance. If PTSD has been a part of your life, either directly or through family and friends, this short but compelling work provides insights into its nature and how one Marine has learned to deal with it. You will find the Poems and the Epilogue as moving as his Odyssey."

Ken Marineau, US Navy, Vietnam

PTSD
and
Expressive Writing

PTSD
and
Expressive Writing

Ending the War Within

by

Brenton MacKinnon

Contact the author at:
brentonmack@yahoo.com

Bookstand Publishing
www.BookstandPublishing.com

Published by
Bookstand Publishing
Morgan Hill, CA 95037
3589_2

978-1-61863-180-0

Printed in the United States of America

DEDICATION

For Jacob

Our heroic WWII veteran who attended
VN vet group therapy sessions as
ordered by the criminal court!
(His story: "Time Bomb")

ACKNOWLEDGEMENTS

In gratitude and memory of the one hundred and seventy one men and boys of Foxtrot Company, 2nd Battalion, 5th Marine Regiment who did not make it home to share their own stories.

INTRODUCTION

Three thousand years ago, Greek warriors returned home after ten years of fighting the Trojan War. As their ships arrived in mainland ports, veterans began making their way back to Athens, city states, villages and farms. These men brought something very special with them, something only they could offer: the spoils of war.

Carved upon their bodies, stamped upon their souls and branded in the memory of survivors they carried the news, information, gossip and descriptions of what lie beyond the known world. Neighbors, safe, bored and starved for excitement competed for the presence of returning warriors as they wined, dined and begged soldiers and sailors for just one more – story.

Gradually and through this constant down loading and debriefing, the psychic baggage carried by combatants was unpacked and its contents spread open to be shared and examined by all. Ten years of accumulated stories were distributed throughout Greece. Fathers, sons and husbands returned not as strangers and outsiders but as story tellers who not only entertained but informed civilians of their personal journey and transformational odyssey.

Here in America combatants and civilian victims of trauma are invited to share the intimate details of combat or abuse during individual and group therapy sessions. We tell part of our story in a circle of survivors with the same type of psychic injury and they listen empathetically. Time is up. Patients return to communities, families, jobs and friends who know nothing of the missing years and hear very little what happened to their citizen soldiers who have returned so deeply changed. They may never know. Is it any wonder that many veterans return and are destined to remain strangers and outsiders?

Combatants from every conflict in the last seventy years weave together a not so magic carpet ride back to this once familiar land of ours. Most find an in-between world of limbo and hover above a landing zone, stranded without a signal beacon to guide them all the way back.

Our newest generation of American veterans is still on patrol. Discharged men and women are struggling and stumbling without a map to find their way home. More are on the way...

While the majority of our warriors return without physical injury, the catastrophic nature of war often results in soul destruction: psychological and emotional collateral damage. Lifelong symptoms can ruin individual character and remove citizen soldiers from contributing to the political, economic and domestic well being of communities.

Our military does offer two very useful PCL-M check lists for personnel about to leave active duty; the first in-country after debriefing sessions and another personal survey at the end of discharge lectures on a U.S. base. Every combatant now knows the wrong answers result in delayed release and psychological evaluation. Anxious to return to families and to avoid the career threatening label of a PTSD diagnosis, they check off the appropriate boxes and get on the bus.

Initially vets do try to fit into civilian life but as symptoms and behaviors develop a destructive life style or a sudden and challenging life crisis are often the results. In spite of a PR campaign by the Veterans Administration claiming 'expanded and improved' programs for those wounded both in mind and body, the waiting list is long and qualification for treatment is challenging and contentious. The best support for returning troops continues to be Vet Centers staffed by professionally trained veteran counselors. No one is turned away but these clinics are few and minimally funded.

Daily suicide rates for active duty personnel and veterans escalate as they suffer the consequences of multiple tours, fail to reintegrate emotionally, find no work, join the homeless population and represent a disproportionate number of those incarcerated.

New agencies and nonprofit groups frequently administered by veterans do provide a variety of imaginative and deeply personal approaches to healing the soul of combatants and families lucky enough to find their way into these retreats, residential programs and long term counseling arrangements.

Whatever path a spiritually wounded veteran may travel, he or she must one day reconcile with the wounded Self within who is still out there in the desert or jungle. At some point each survivor must do the work, often alone and negotiate if not unconditional peace, a cease fire.

What *can* be done by a veteran yet to enter the VA system, placed on a wait-list and in emotional isolation after the first weeks, months and even years after returning to civilian life? How can warriors connect with family, friends and neighbors who expect veterans to behave as though they have returned unchanged?

You hold one possibility in your hands. The value of expressive writing for combat veterans suffering from PTSD is well documented and shows measureable results in lessening the severity of both physiological and psychological symptoms.

I was diagnosed in 1995 with PTSD. Self help manuals, medications, counselors, group therapy and a psychiatrist came and went. It wasn't until my foxhole buddy, Sgt. David Anderson, suggested I write a researched and annotated, non-fiction autobiography that real healing began.

It took a year and as I reached the end something began to change and move within me: I resisted completing the memoir. Why? I knew instinctively that the writing process would reframe both selective and subjective memories by providing an actual time line of events with the full names of comrades and an ordered and sequential history from the unit diary. As I wrote the last line and prepared to share the story with friends and family, not only would my memory of the past be different but it would also affect how I experienced daily life as a civilian in the present.

Most importantly, those around me would now know my story and through the telling, know that the person who had left for war did come home deeply transformed but willing to announce, "This is my story. This is what happened. This is who I am. I want to come home."

Bravery is necessary during wartime. Back home, emotional courage and behavioral changes are more difficult, especially when familiar habits pull one back into a safer but often dysfunctional comfort zone.

You are about to read a collection of short stories and poems, each a small step forward as I sought peace within. Conversations are shared with warriors, sometimes from other cultures with similar wounds. And yes, even with men who were sworn enemies from a time and place where no mercy was expected or given: Vietnam.

Expressive Writing can and does help us find our way back. I teach this subject now and in the following pages you will read a story of my first day in class as both instructor and wounded veteran. You will see: my own journey continues.

This book is an example of what many vets are writing all across America. We hope that you will pick up the pen and by doing so gradually heal the wounds caused by the sword. Join a Vet Center program, register for a creative writing class or find a manual for personal and guided journaling. If you can't locate a local program and need an alternative, please feel free to email me: brentonmack@yahoo.com.

Writing is between you and – you. Personal inhibition often found in private counseling sessions or groups is not present when alone at your desk or kitchen table. Your conversation is with you. New thoughts, memories and feelings often surface and are captured and articulated for the first time on a piece of paper.

You are not the same person who left for WWII, Korea, Iraq, Afghanistan or Vietnam. When ready, the sharing of a memoir, a poem or a short story with family and friends brings new understanding of the returning warrior. His or her reintroduction into community will begin with those who have been waiting to hear what happened and who we are now.

After publishing my memoir, civilian and military friends from the past and present contacted me to share their own experiences of trauma, grief and emotional healing. Acceptance, inclusion and intimacy is being known.

As you write each new page, that part of you still 'in-country' can turn in a new direction to begin the necessary inner journey and come all the way back home.

Pick up the pen. Take the first step…

TABLE OF CONTENTS

PTSD and Expressive Writing

Part I
Language

The call to adventure arrived, not in the classic form of a wizard offering a quest or the ghost of Hamlet's dead father demanding revenge but through the feudal tradition of the military draft. An M-16 replaced a knight's lance, Bubba from Biloxi masqueraded as Sir Galahad and small yellow guerillas in the jungle appeared in the role of berserking, dyed blue men descending from the heather of the Scottish Highlands terrorizing Roman legions along Hadrian's Wall.

By 1966, more than a decade had passed since the battles of Pork Chop Hill and Heartbreak Ridge in the Korea War. Prosperity followed; men orbited the Earth and a new generation of boys grew up with comics, movies and toy guns. Once again, America had forgotten. Once again, young men were restless.

Faraway places and cultures? A rowdy band of hormonal brothers drafted and volunteering from fifty different States and the territories? Your own automatic rifle with notches to notch? The Wild West! (In this case the Wild East.) Why not? Our many battles, fought inside books and movies as knights, soldiers, space men, cowboys and Sioux Indians obviously qualified our generation for the heroics of combat.

My own linguistic skills acquired in a comic book jungle as Tarzan's bilingual sidekick resulted in a language aptitude test with the Marine Corps and qualified me for the Army Defense Language Institute. I passed the course and soon felt noblesse oblige for the monolingual Marines in my staging unit. How could I have known that a four month language course would not only save my life many times over but lay the foundation for a lifelong career?

Just what is the value of acquiring a second language? Consider: You are in a Mexican restaurant, a Vietnamese fingernail salon or maybe a Parisian bistro. The foreign born staff converse in some unintelligible language, laugh and look your way. In our inability to understand, self assurance dissolves, quickly replaced by suspicion, insecurity and often anger. "They're laughing at me!" (In Paris they probably are.)

A second language expands our universe, our ability to put ourselves in someone else's shoes, creates deeper understanding of the cultural forces shaping 'foreigners' and builds bridges with next door neighbors here at home. Bilingualism opens a two way door for both participants and also carries cultural information in a conversation. Our preconceptions, imaginings and even prejudicial states of mind often evaporate or in some cases are validated though understanding rather than assumption.

Knowledge of the enemy's language during wartime doubles sensitivity, awareness and paranoia. After seven months in combat as an interpreter and two months living alone in a remote village, the bi-cultural world around me slowly blended together. I began to think, dream and feel in both Vietnamese and English.

During the second half of my tour, two languages and living with Vietnamese messed me up good, all because of language training. Patriotism and politics grew fuzzy as my perspective moved back and forth between two populations, different versions of right and wrong, good and bad and ultimately, imperialist troops vs. freedom fighting nationalists. Boundaries of self identity and criteria for decision making shifted with each new crisis, daily appeals from terrorized villagers and orders from the often out of touch battalion command.

I began to wonder: On which side of the barbed wire did I belong?

The Albino Gorilla

"If I can teach a parrot to sing "God Save the Queen, "I can certainly teach this savage a thing or two."

Tarzan of the Apes
Edgar R. Burroughs

"What do you call someone who speaks many languages?"

"I don't know."

"Multilingual!"

"How about someone who speaks two languages?"

"Bilingual?"

"Right."

"One language?"

I sat pondering so he answered for me.

"American!"

Sergei slapped me on the shoulder and my tumbler of vodka almost spilled. All the Soviets in the small apartment laughed and while I watched these new best friends celebrate, I wondered what twist of fate had deposited me in far away Kazakhstan, drinking with soldiers just returned from Afghanistan. Why wasn't I selling insurance in Los Angeles or on some mainstream career track?

I tossed the vodka down and saw Sergei's face through the bottom of the glass. A youthful twenty year old rascal, he looked like my fifth grade pal, Chuck...

...Los Angeles, 1955, back before it was messed up. Huge bean fields had survived a few blocks away from our neighborhood and held the trees and streams where my prepubescent buddies and I hunted jackrabbits with bow and arrow. We called this last cloister of wild sanctuary, "The Jungle". Our tribe built rafts, camped out, cooked, ruled the unexplored lands and chased off explorers.

Why "The Jungle" you ask? Before color TV and multimedia we subscribed to, read and traded comic books. Each month when Chuck's new copy of Tarzan arrived we fled to the privacy of his backyard tree house to slowly unwrap the Holy Scripture.

There he was! On the cover: swinging through the trees, wrestling with a lion or battling a tribe of cannibals.

Chuck and I read aloud and acted out scenarios, scripts and mythological characters fifteen feet off the ground just like The Lord of the Jungle. You no doubt remember great apes had adopted Tarzan and one day he would become not only their leader but also protector of the jungle and traditional family values.

How did Tarzan communicate with his gorilla buddies? Why, he spoke ape of course. Every other month the Tarzan comic published an Ape-English dictionary on the last page. Chuck and I memorized every word and this, dear reader, is responsible not only for my many visits to the principal's office but for tossing down vodka ten thousand miles away from what might have been a safe and snug little cubical in the City of the Angels.

As Chuck and I approached fluency in Ape Talk, we decided to flaunt our sophistication on the playground during recess at Westchester Elementary

School. Rain did not dampen our excitement as we stood below the overhang of the outdoor cafeteria. Leroy, the Bully, and dominant ape, patrolled his domain and scanned No Man's Land for potential victims. Swept away by linguistic revelry, Chuck accidentally looked Leroy in the eye!

Someone else spoke through me, using my mouth. "Kreegah abalu!" (Beware brother!)

In monosyllabic joy, Leroy turned his wrath on me. "Hey girl! You want this?" His fist was quite large for our age group.

Behind him, Chuck screamed. "Bundolo togoni!" (Kill baboon)

Leroy did not score well in recent academic testing. "Hunh?"

In a flash of brilliance Chuck demanded. "Kagoda manu?" (Do you surrender monkey?)

Giggling from the girls gathered around us wilted poor Leroy and my fear of imminent death evaporated. What power! Chuck and I had authored a new playground scenario spoken in a mystical tongue from the Dark Continent.

We pulled on imaginary leopard skins and soon the plastered walls of school transformed into thatched huts as we explored a whole new land. Answering questions in class, intimidating monolingual speakers at recess, Tarzan 'talking' all day long, ah, the sweet taste of saying just what you want at any time with no consequences!

Teachers, friends and janitors were not amused. Eleven year old kids have no power of course. Adults, as they must, intervened and conspired, then relocated

Chuck and me to different fifth grade rooms. Left with the loneliness only the truly gifted know, repatriation to my English speaking tribe of commoners left me isolated, just another alienated refugee. At the end of the semester we all immigrated to the distant continent of Puberty: middle school.

Airport Junior High School had initiated and launched the first bussing program in Los Angeles. As the accordion doors of yellow buses squeezed open, brown-skinned students swarmed onto our white bread turf. I knew then that Tarzan of the Apes had not abandoned me. Spanish came easily that I soon enjoyed the first cross-cultural romance in our school with Ramona Ramirez.

We did kiss… once.

Seems I still enjoyed the raw instincts and aptitude acquired in The Jungle. Our military sent me to study Vietnamese at the Defense Language Institute. The Peace Corps taught me French in the Sahara Desert. Fijian classes were necessary in a construction project…other languages followed.

I think of Chuck now and then. We actually wrote a comic book of our own but as we were pure linguists, not artists, it did not receive the attention it deserved.

…Back in Kazakhstan, Sergei stood and demanded, "More vodka my capitalist brother! Another bottle and you will be speaking Russian!"

What would Tarzan do? Still looking for my magical tribe, I slid the tumbler across the table and the imagined space separating us grew smaller.

"What are they gonna do? Send me to Vietnam?"
Refrain of Vietnam bound
troops contemplating
a questionable act

Three Part Harmony
Defense Language Institute

The graduation party was going well; Chinese food for eighteen in downtown Monterey, California. Our officer in charge, whom we called Lieutenant Numbnuts, stood and assumed credit for our academic achievements as a result of his due diligence and motivation. After the war, studying with the U.S. Army would be remembered as my easiest tour of duty while serving with the Marine Corps.

We had arrived four months earlier on a Greyhound bus from Camp Pendleton, four hours before our transit orders expired at midnight. Ten Marines stood on the sidewalk with ten duffle bags at 8 PM in a tourist town. What to do? As senior enlisted man by a week, I ordered the squad to shoulder bags and march in formation to the nearest bar.

We found a circular glassed-in pub overlooking the yacht harbor. With instincts that were to serve me well in combat, I scouted out two retired Marines sitting in a booth. They waved us over and bought all the drinks. Time passed.

Ten minutes before midnight, we all poured out of taxis at the top of Presidio Hill and reported to a sleepy desk sergeant. Drunk and rowdy had little impact on him as the only other Marines of his acquaintance must have served in WWII movies.

Early next morning after roll call, our designated Officer In Charge, Lt. Numbnuts, roostered an inspirational speech. "Your aptitude scores indicate you are the best Camp Pendleton has to offer – at this time. Obviously, you can acquire Vietnamese in four months. If you do not, you are shit birds will be prosecuted for dereliction of duty. Not go get some chow and don't embarrass me or you will regret it."

Yes, ten guinea pig Marines. If we successfully demonstrated that enlisted Marines could actually learn, (an issue much discussed by the other armed services) more and larger groups would follow.

We soon found out the Army really did know how to motivate! Six classes, six hours a day, six days a week, taught by young, attractive Vietnamese women. Pride in early progress faded when Army pals over some brews at the Enlisted Club revealed that our teachers' approval was actually, fear of failure. As Vietnamese nationals their administrator would lose face and return them not only to a far less privileged lifestyle back home but to civil war. No one ever failed a test in their classes or gotten laid. (The only possible explanation was that they were holding out for an officer and citizenship.)

Meanwhile, our graduation party needed lubrication. My two bottles of Orange Flavored Eden Roc set me back almost five bucks.

"Give me some of that wine you got under the table, Mac."

"OK Jimmie, but give Ron some."

"Of course, Dipshit."

My fellow wine connoisseurs from South Texas knew the vintage well. Using evasion tactics learned during infantry training, our three Chinese teacups moved back and forth under the table like a boat of refugees landing under the cover of darkness.

Crinkling of the paper bag went unnoticed amidst laughter and conversation around the banquet table. Still seated inside the Golden Duck Palace, the three of us were soon transported to Eden and my natural leadership qualities surfaced despite a year of military discipline.

Graduation would separate our holy trinity. The first group of ten Marines sent to the famous Defense Language Institute graduated! Had we enlisted Marines performed well and acquired a second language? No one really knew. For instructors it was either give us all a passing score or get on a plane and fly eight thousand miles to the war zone with us. War is Hell. Five of our group and their twangy South Texas accents butchered the tonal Vietnamese language.

Jimmy got a C. Once in country he and the other Texans were reassigned as grunts where their grunting of Vietnamese did not alienate the hearts and minds of local villagers. Yes, we had all passed and not burned the place down. Time to celebrate!

I turned away from flirting with the cute female teachers and scouted for Chinese targets of opportunity. A souvenir perhaps? Under the pretense of complementing the cooks, I left the table and pushed through swinging double doors to the kitchen. Jimmy followed along and behind him the manager, wringing his hands. Fuck it. What were they going to do? Send me us Vietnam?

I chatted up the cooks while circling the kitchen and searching for a possible candidate. Of course! There, shining and glittering and calling out to me, the classical weapon of choice for a warrior: a meat cleaver!

"Jimmy, distraction."

We had faced similar challenges. Magically, a plate of food fell off the prep table and crashed on the tile floor. As a highly trained guerilla fighter, I smoothly slid the cleaver under my tunic and walked back to the banquet room while Jimmy took the Chinese heat.

Still high on vitamin C from orange wine, Ron, Jimmy and I walked back up Presidio Hill to the school. Just as on our first night, the midnight bell from the old Spanish mission echoed from the town below. Reaching the top of the hill, we saw It.

Erected on the grassy knoll by the rear entrance to the dorm, stood a cardboard Nativity scene. Spotlights stuck in the grass highlighted three figures looming over an unsuspecting family. The wise men, like three opportunistic colonels, stood gazing down at the new draftee in a manger. Joe and Mary looked ready to sign consent papers for enlistment.

Roly-poly baby Jesus, a three dimensional white plastic Pillsbury Dough boy, smiled up at us with his extended umbilical cord running twenty feet to an electrical outlet. Inside his tummy, a light bulb illuminated and expanded his aura into the night and holiday season.

Poor guy. Jesus was to suffer the same fate as four Marines from our language class, but while they fell in obscure forests and jungles, Jesus suffered through the most publicized public death ever recorded. As a Marine, I couldn't leave him behind.

With prophetic foresight, the mission became crystal clear. The meat cleaver. An instant later, the heads of the Three Colonels lay on the ground, no longer a threat to the underage recruit.

Jesus Christ, Mac!" Ron was Catholic.

"Exactly. Unplug that extension cord." I grabbed Jesus and stuck him inside the huge doggie bag we'd hauled all the way back from the restaurant.

"Let's go."

"No shit." Jimmy fired only one or two words in burst. Trained as a machine gunner, he saved his ammo.

Back at the dorm room, our over achier Ron paced back and forth. "Holy shit. They'll know it's us. They'll search our rooms and I'll get busted."

I'd already lost a stripe for coming in late and a bit tipsy." I reassured him. "It doesn't hurt."

"Put him back! There's still time before the MPs do the 0200 check."

This seemed too good an opportunity to waste. "OK, you go back to your room. I swear He will return to the manger in a few minutes."

What would Jesus do? That great guy who had embraced all mankind. Ah, yes. Thanks to Eden Roc Winery and the Marine Corps with men and women from every ethnic group in America, my own light bulb lit up.

Next morning, the cafeteria buzzed and hummed like a beehive with overdressed bees. The few black brothers eating in the corner together seemed particularly animated.

Lt. Numbnuts separated from his little group of the officer elite and marched over, no doubt to wish us bon voyage and well done.

A hand on his hip was one of his favorite poses. "What time did you shit birds sign in last night?

Ron had the most practice at playing it straight. "The Sarge was asleep at the desk with his head down on the clipboard, so we just went on up."

I got the feeling he didn't believe us and I didn't look up from Snap, Crackle, and Pop laughing in my cereal bowl.

His official leadership voice barked. "Some asshole vandalized the nativity scene last night. He painted shoe black on the face and extremities of Baby Jesus and plugged him back in. We're lucky it didn't start a riot. I will inspect all your rooms immediately after breakfast!" He did a clumsy about face and marched off to his social equals.

Ron rubbed the newly awarded stripe on his shoulder. "Jesus, Mac."

"Exactly."

*"Behold, how good and how pleasant it is for
Brethren to dwell together in unity."*

Psalms 133:1

Saved by Translation
An Hoa Valley
Vietnam

In the first week of January, a C130 transport plane dumped me onto the red mud of An Hoa, Vietnam. The 2nd Battalion of the 5th Marine Regiment ran patrols and sweeps into "Indian Country" and rotated one infantry company each month to stand security on top of Nong Son Mountain, two miles away.

Excited and nervous, I stood at attention in front of the Battalion First Sergeant ready for assignment as a specialist in interrogation or intelligence. He shuffled through my file for a few seconds and handed it back to me.

"OK Private, go on over to Fox Company. They need riflemen."

A grunt? A common rifleman? I didn't move.

He turned back to the tall stack of paper on his desk. Overworked and worn out, he paused and stared up at me. "What are you waiting for Private?"

"First Sergeant, I don't know if you noticed but I attended Vietnamese language school."

He stood. "We don't need no fuckin' gook talkers. We need riflemen. Now get the fuck over there!"

As a new member of the 1st Platoon I kept my mouth shut and tried to learn from more experienced grunts how to survive. After a month of patrols, ambushes, sand bagging, operations, and sleep deprivation, Hugh Hefner intervened on my behalf.

Local Vietnamese militia officers invited our company commander to meet and discuss collaboration at a local village. A few days later, Fox Company encircled the selected site and as I walked by with my squad, the gunny pulled two of us out to stand guard duty in front of a grass hut.

Gunny Jones grumbled, "Keep your shit together. The Colonel's comin over from An Hoa for the meeting inside. Don't fuck up!"

Me and Rabbi shrugged and assumed what we thought to be intimidating foreign devil personas on each side of the door. Time passed so we started bullshitting and relaxed. Villagers noticed we had dissolved into human beings and curious, approached.

"Rabbi, watch this. I'll blow their minds."

I turned and faced the dozen or so villagers. "Chao cac Ong. Manh gioi?" (Howdy everybody. How are you?)

The crowd laughed and moved closer. A foreign devil spoke Vietnamese and with a terrible and comical accent.

Rabbi stiffened. "Jesus, Mac! What the fuck did you say?"

"Shalom."

"Well, tell em to move back! What's that guy in the back pullin out?" Rabbi released the safety on his M16.

"Lai dei!" I called the man forward.

""It's Playboy Magazine, Rabbi."

The villager opened his magazine and showed me a full page cartoon. "Cai nai la cai yi?" (This thing is what thing?)

It took five minutes to explain the cultural concept of pictorial humor. In an effort to win hearts and minds, I began to interpret the cartoon jokes. Soon, thirty villagers gathered in front of us laughing and howling as I translated captions.

"What the hell is going on here?"

Rabbi and I snapped to attention. Our Colonel came around from behind the hut with his bodyguards.

"Uh, Sir. I was just translating these Playboy jokes for the folks here, Sir."

"How the hell do you speak Vietnamese son?"

"Sir, I attended DLI in Monterey."

"What's your job with Foxtrot, Private?"

"Rifleman, Sir."

"Come with me."

We entered the darkened hut with six allied officers sitting on the ground.

The Colonel interrupted, "Captain Graham, did you know this Marine speaks Vietnamese and is assigned as a rifleman in your company? If you don't use him appropriately, I will take him back with me to Battalion."

"Colonel, I didn't know. We'll bring him into the CP as an interpreter."

"Damn right you will." Our battalion commanding officer turned to me. "Now introduce our new friends here." He grabbed my arm. "Son, you sit next to me and make sure they don't bullshit us."

"Yes, Sir."

As the source of his discomfort, I tried not to look at Captain Graham. My life had just changed forever and thanks to the universal appeal of Playboy Magazine, I was to eventually return home. 1st Platoon was to suffer many casualties…

"Music is one of the ways we can achieve a kind of shorthand to understand each other."

Yo Yo Ma

The Sound of Music
Quang Tri
1967

"No Mac, I'm tellin' you. It was Jackie Wilson not Wilson Picket who sang that song." Robby unfolded a can opener from the C-ration box and pulled out a can of ham and Lima beans. Lunchtime at our observation post.

I looked over my shoulder at the tree line across the long dry rice paddy and returned to our long running debate: Motown.

"You think because I'm white I don't have a memory?"

Robby stared at the last lima bean inside the can as though it was Frank Sinatra's photo on a record label. He looked over at me, sweat glistening on his black skin.

"You still don't get it. You're OK, Mac, for a California boy and lucky enough to have a soul station to listen to while you were safe in your suburb. But music is a cultural thing, Brother, something in the blood, and well, your blood is yours and ours and ours.

We finished eating in silence. We knew the color of blood by then.

"It's time to call in. Check it out, Mac."

I put my can of mixed fruit down and scanned the tree line with binoculars. Nothing. Plastic on the handset was hot so I held it away from my ear and squeezed the button. The rest of the company had dug in for lunch maybe two hundred meters behind us.

"Foxtrot Four. This is OP One. Over."

Static, then Smitty's Southern twang. "Copy. Go."

"Sitrep. All clear. Over."

"Roger. Out." Smitty clicked off.

"Hey Mac, give me that can of mixed fruit and I'll sing the whole song for you and you can admit you're blowing smoke about Wilson Pickett."

"I know the lyrics, Robby and my voice is better."

"Bullshit! I heard you sing."

"Listen to this." I stood up, took a deep breath and opened my mouth. Nothing came out.

Halfway across the rock hard paddy in front of us, fifty to sixty guerillas were running at full speed. Metal flashed in the sun.

"Holy fuck! Let's go!" I slipped the radio on my back, triggered the phone, and started running.

"Foxtrot Four. OP One. Fifty VC, half a click out moving in. Don't fire!"

The radio weighed twenty five pounds and after fifty meters, Robby began to leave me behind. Hot and humid, big dirt clods everywhere, I began to slow down. Robbie stopped. He turned and sank to one knee. The M16 came up and he emptied a clip alongside my ear back toward our observation post.

"Come on, Mac!"

He slapped another clip in and that's when we heard it, chopper blades. Robby pointed above the tree line on the south side of the paddy.

"Fuckin' a! They're makin' a run on us! They think we're VC."

A Cobra gunship on nearby air support lined up for a strafing run two hundred meters out and was coming fast. From the air all combatants looked the same ... but not quite.

I laid down on my stomach and called in. "Foxtrot. Abort chopper. Friendlies!"

Static.

"Abort! Abort!"

Nothing.

Robby stared at me. I shook my head.

The gunship closed to a hundred meters. Robby stood up, unbuckled his helmet and threw it down. He turned his dark face up to the oncoming chopper and an arm went up with the middle finger thrust into the Vietnamese sky.

He screamed. "I'm Black you Muthafucker! Black!"

The Cobra pulled up, swooped over us and turned around to reacquire another target: the front line of the VC assault.

"Forget the radio, Mac!"

We jumped up and waving our arms in the air, sprinted to the outer ring of the company defensive position. No one shot us so we ran inside the circle and dove behind a blasted-out tree stump. Relieved, exhausted and exhilarated, we laughed while around us, Foxtrot opened fire. Hearts pounding together and gasping for air, we leaned side by side against the stump.

"I have never been so happy to be so Black in

all my Godamned life!"

"Me too Robby, me too."

He turned to me and smiled with beauty I still see, "It *was* Jackie Wilson, you know."

Part II
The Sword

March 1967: Quang Nam Province caught fire. People began to die with regularity and the fog of my civilian existentialism evaporated. Both terrifying and exhilarating, the world around me shifted into colored coded, black and white. Enemy tried to kill us and we tried to kill them. No confusion, no bullshit, no speculation.

The official KIA list for Foxtrot Company holds one hundred and seventy one dead, the equivalent of two wartime infantry companies. Failure to pay attention and behave properly resulted in death for one's self and frequently, others. We lived a violent utopia of co-dependency and brotherhood. Petty differences of race, education, and rank dissolved with the first incoming round. My need to belong to a community sharing the same consciousness, cooperation and commitment had arrived with a high price tag.

Yet, Ernest Hemmingway haunted me. Like a bullfighter facing the moment of truth, I had yet to experience epiphany in that second before death, that flash of illumination in which the secret of the Great Mystery is revealed. On June 2, 1967 the crack in the universe opened and answered my unspoken prayer.

"They use their instinctive sense of observation to help others in times of need and are among the most fit of all the Animal signs to survive most any situation."

The Rat
Chinese Astrology

The Rat Whisperer
Phu Loc Outpost

"Mac, you sleep in the communication bunker tonight and man both radios. Cowboy is out on ambush."

"Gunny, he told me there's a big rat in there that runs around in the dark."

"Just leave a couple of C-ration cans open near the entrance when you hit the rack. We got him trained."

"OK."

Two radios stood on top of some wooden crates in the corner. Overhead, a light bulb dangled down from bare wires hooked up to a jeep battery. Rows of leaky sandbags dribbled streams of sand with every vibration echo from eighty millimeter mortars firing illumination rounds for the patrols down by the river. Spooky. Like the inside of a large intestine with ulcers bleeding sand.

I threw my pack on top of the cot and sat on three ammo cans stacked in front of the radios. Gunny bent down and stuck his head through the doorway. "You can sleep after 2400 but turn the volume up and wear headphones."

"What's the name of the operation tomorrow?"

"Dixie. You are on the first APC* with the radio. Routine. Red will be here at 0600 to brief you on secure frequencies and codes."

"Where we goin'?'"

"Across the river and through all the local villes. Show of force." He turned and spit tobacco juice on the red soil. "Scare the shit out of 'em."

"OK, Gunny."

Life as company radioman kept me in the flow of info. As part of the CP* and surrounded by three platoons of riflemen, we only engaged the enemy in moments of chaos and imminent disaster. Radio was a much better job than my previous role as rifleman where the only source of information was barking by Sgt. Henderson.

On Dixie, my radio and I would ride on top of a motorized personnel carrier, call in and pass along check points by the flanking squads outside the column. The best part? Yelling down at former squad members in 1st Platoon ground pounding their way through red mud.

Around 1900 hours I got hungry. Under the moldy cot, empty boxes of C-rats competed for space with a new case. I bent down to make my selection. The top of the case was gone, along with every box except one last, "Beans and Wieners." Someone had looted the contents and no doubt traded it down in the ville for contraband or pussy.

When you're hungry, even cold franks and beans taste good. Special packets of cheese and crackers, a mini chocolate bar and everyone's favorite of pound cake. Cold instant coffee topped off the feast.

24

Ten minutes later, I wired the empty cans together in the doorway as an alarm. Sappers had penetrated the smaller outpost down the road some weeks before and everyone was more paranoid than usual.

Cardboard on top of the ammo can chair softened my butt as patrols called in from checkpoints every fifteen minutes. After midnight, they set up ambush scenarios and radio silence followed until dawn or until the shit hit the fan.

I spun the dial looking for Vietnamese radio conversations and chipped in with some juicy swear words learned from our Vietnamese scouts. The gooks went ape shit. Sometimes out of boredom, I called our own platoon radiomen and spoke Vietnamese just to mind fuck 'em. Gotta keep 'em alert.

Midnight came around and I unscrewed the light bulb, grabbed the headphones and got comfy on the cot. The occasional popping of illumination flares, random gunshots, and the dull hum of high level aircraft serenaded me to sleep...

In my dream, Lynne and I danced the last dance at our high school prom. We melted together, each holding the promise of a sweet night to follow. Someone tapped my arm trying to cut in. I ignored him. Probably that asshole, Algie with the red Plymouth Fury convertible. He tapped again, harder. I held Lynne tighter. Pain. A knife pierced my left bicep. I screamed!

Back in the bunker, someone had hold of my bicep with a pair of pliers and twisted. I reached across to beat him off with my fist and pounded into fur. The bunker rat wouldn't let go so I pulled my pistol from its holster and fired a shot into the sandbag wall.

He finally scurried away, no doubt to rejoin his communist trainer. Alarm cans rattled and a flashlight beam speared me from the open doorway.

"What the fuck's goin on in here? You got the whole perimeter on lock and load!"

"It was the rat, Gunny. He took a chunk out of my arm. I left the cans out like you said." His light moved down and tracked the empty cans on the wire.

"Dipshit! You're supposed to leave food in the damn cans! He bit you 'cause he's pissed. Just like me! Now I gotta send you back to Battalion for rabies shots. How the fuck am I gonna train another radioman in three fuckin' hours?"

"I'll do it."

"Damn right you will. I'll send Doc over to stop that bleeding and get someone from 2nd Platoon for the radio. Don't fuck up."

"Yes, Gunny." (The guy loved me.)

The light bulb lit up the bunker again. I wrapped a rag around my bicep and set up the radios for a lesson. I felt someone behind me and I turned to see a skinny kid standing under a helmet. He looked about twelve.

"Come on in and pull up an ammo can. What's your name?

"Bobby Jackson. I came in with the replacements last week. Went to com school back in Pendleton, so Gunny sent me over. Sorry about your bite. Think you'll get a Purple Heart?"

He learned everything I could teach in about ten

26

minutes so I let him play with the frequencies, dial up radio watch back at Battalion and talk radio talk.

Doc came and I spent the last few hours before dawn in his tent. Right on schedule, two APCs roared up just after sunrise. Jackson crawled up on top of the first one with our flamethrower team, smiling all the while like he was riding a float in a parade.

I yelled up, "Don't trash my lucky radio. Took a week to get a new battery."

"OK, Mac." Jesus. In daylight, I could see he had buckteeth.

A convoy with two platoons of grunts and the APCs left through the opening in the concertina wire and rumbled off down the road heading for the river.

"Mac! Get your shit and jump on the resupply chopper when it turns around. Two weeks goofin' off back there with rear shit birds. Hope they make you burn the shit."

"Yes, Gunny."

Fourteen rabies shots had a bad reputation. But a new vaccine injected subcutaneously and didn't torture as advertised. Gunny would be disappointed. Since I had to report to the hospital shed every day, my rear job as gopher for the place went smoothly until the second day.

Three medivac choppers landed on the helipad carrying casualties from Operation Dixie. Overhead, another copter flew east in the direction of graves registration.

"Grab a gurney and follow me!" Commander Viti led the way.

First off H34 bird was a burn victim from the

flamethrower team. Doc Viti shot him up with morphine until the screaming stopped. Hard to tell with the burns and all but he looked like Tony from the flame team.

"Tony. It's me, Mac. What happened?"

Through groans and tears, he told the story. "Our APC hit a mine and the diesel fuel tank exploded. Blew me into the river. The rest of them didn't make it. Only me."

Thankfully, he passed out. Viti yelled at the chopper pilot through the cockpit side window. "Got enough fuel for Da Nang? OK. Take this guy to MAC5 trauma unit."

We loaded Tony back on the H34, watched it lift off and fly east towards the coast. The rat bite started to burn. I rubbed my arm and started thinking how things played out.

Much has changed in the last forty-two years since Vietnam. I still haven't figured out much. Shit happens, or doesn't. Bobby Jackson never made it to nineteen and part of me never made it home. But each year on the night before Memorial Day, I open up a can of gourmet beef, leave it on the back porch, and salute Brother Rat.

In the morning… it's all gone.

*armored personnel carrier

28

"One man with courage makes a majority."

Saying

The Gladiator's Voice
Battle of Union II
June 2, 1967

I transferred to the small CP (Command Personnel) as company radioman, translator and as ordered by the Gunny, to trade my life for Captain Graham's if necessary: I was "replaceable", our Captain was not. During the daylight hours and until the day he died on June 2, I was his constant companion, shadow and relay voice to our platoons and weapons people. We came to know each other well.

My first impression of Jim Graham was one of mental instability. His enthusiasm for combat was child-like, yet his physical appearance was intense, lean, and hungry. Some predator caged in the same body had escaped into his own personal hunting ground: Vietnam. A large hooked nose dominated his features. He often reminded me of a hawk.

He was one of the rare ones; thriving in the most difficult of circumstances, spirit soaring, senses electric and dancing skillfully with the shadow of death hovering above An Hoa. Most of us in Foxtrot Company just wanted to go home.

The Captain looked much older than his 26 years. He had a serious demeanor yet practiced a compassionate humor with everyone and enjoyed an especially good rapport with fellow officers and NCO staff. Respected, courageous and popular, he continuously studied situation reports, maps, personnel and reviews of intelligence flowing from various sources. He was, as the saying goes, "Born Ready."

We all felt he was the best possible commander in the most difficult of times. An aggressive and tactical leader, he enabled Foxtrot to gain a few victories in the midst of chaos and attrition. We had pride in our company and ourselves.

At the time, it appeared that Captain Graham's personal mission was not the promotion ladder. For him, combat was the opportunity of a lifetime: Field Commander. He lusted after contact, engagement, battle and all this he pursued at every chance. My single reservation? I felt he believed that he had been anointed to embrace a special destiny and this would one day lead us to destruction. It was not ambition per se but a powerful inner force which others felt and interpreted each in our own way.

Over time, I came to respect Captain Graham's obsessive habits as these made all of us better warriors. He inspired confidence. We saw other companies come and go and suffer casualties through horrendous mistakes. He was disciplined both professionally and privately.

He carried a Bible and toilet articles in the field when no one else did. He changed fatigues in the middle of nowhere. We were grungy. He washed, shaved, brushed his teeth and put on pressed fatigues; always ready and always at his best.

In those days, I saw him as an archetype, living out an almost messianic vision. Each day he put on his robes, performed his absolutions and said his prayers. He was, I felt, ready to die at all times. This impression, I came to understand in later years, was of a man fully prepared to live and function in the present moment.

Yet all around him we enlisted men felt the war was a sham and not worth dying for. I feared Graham would one day lead us into the Valley of Death for absolutely no reason.

That day finally arrived on June 2, 1967. A long, dry rice paddy lay before us and a ripple of apprehension traveled through the entire company. For the first time I witnessed Graham hesitate and then question the order given to him by Colonel Hilgartner of the 1st Battalion 5th Regiment to advance. Our Captain had good reasons. There was evidence to suggest formidable enemy forces were waiting in the tree line across the paddy. And indeed, they were…

Captain Jim Graham *was* courageous when the time came; not with guns blazing to assault and destroy but in a doomed effort to save our people in the Second Platoon, ambushed in the rice paddy. His voice still echoes across the decades, "Every man with a rifle, follow me!"

He was an authentic hero, a caring person who did the right thing at the right time and sacrificed himself in an impossible situation.

The last time I saw Jim Graham he laid dead on a poncho. He had given everything in the face of certain death. For me and many other survivors, our family died that day. Our Captain was gone and with him the heart and soul of Foxtrot.

"And that had he told them, they would have answered with a shocked, uncomprehending stare."

Icarus
Edward Fields

Talking With the Dead
An Hoa Base

I am a hollow statue wearing a skin of ragged uniform, gear, weapons and dirt. I have no body.

Floating in a bad dream, we few survivors climb down off the helicopters. Zombies in filthy fatigues, some partially clothed some in bandages, others dazed and supported by companions.

Impotent and armed only with a pencil, our Fox Company admin clerk stands counting bodies as we stagger towards the double line of huts and hooches. His name? My mind is numb.

He recognizes me. "Mac!"

I keep moving, going... somewhere.

His lips move again. "Johnson?"

I shake my head.

"Driscoll? The mortar squad?"

A voice moves through me, whispers. "No."

I keep moving. Our hooch looks a thousand meters away and in the same moment, I feel wooden steps under my feet. The screen door squeaks as always, as though nothing has happened. Inside the silent space, cots and footlockers stand squared away, waiting for their Marines.

Lying on his stolen bookshelf are Joe's phonograph and pirated record albums from R&R in

Bangkok. New letters from Driscoll's mom scatter across his rack. Sarge's collection of *Popular Mechanics* remains stacked under his cot. Next to Mike's pillow, a pencil pokes out, saving a place in his poetry notebook.

Our hooch stands ready for their return. Faithful and intimate possessions wait to be brought to life again by human touch. Now these things too are dead, tombstones in a graveyard full of ghosts. Rows of cots like empty coffins await bodies they once comforted. Every one dead. Everyone, but me.

Someone moves off to my left. Who violates this holy ground? With a hand on my pistol and the Evil Eye, I turn and stare down the stranger. An old man, filthy, bearded, with dead eyes stares back.

I confront him. "What the fuck are you look..."

His mouth is open. He moves as I move. I am yelling, challenging a mirror. A stranger. What happened to *me*? The person I remember just a few days ago is no more.

The old man stares back and I see in his eyes a part of me, lying out in that rice paddy in a body bag. I sit down on the end of my cot. I want to cry, need to cry. But there are no tears in this grey shadow land I have entered into.

But I know now: I will survive. They can't kill a ghost.

"I ceased to be a soldier. Only my helmet remained. I found myself without water bottle, rations, gasmask. My watch had lost its cover and glass. An enormous burden of responsibility seemed to roll away as if this were the end off a pilgrim's progress. There was no pain. I felt at rest."

R. H. Tawney
Infantry, WWI

Speechless

"Robby, what happened out there?" Overhead, another barrage of artillery shells raced through the night seeking the North Vietnamese Army position two clicks out. Without a weapon, flak jacket, shirt or helmet he sat staring back the across the dry rice paddy.

"They're all dead." An 80mm parachute flare ignited, swayed back and forth, drifting slowly down over the ambush site. Dark shadows of our friends lay flickering and twitching under the burning star as though they might still be alive, strong enough to crawl to us and safety But the executions squads had done their job and rejoined the NVA regiment in retreat.

"Mac, I gotta tell someone. I'm fucked up. You were out there. You'll believe me."

"What happened to your gear?" All I had left was a 45 pistol found in a back pack as my own group of wounded stumbled back across the red dirt in darkness.

He looked up at a pair of A4's flew low with

another load to let go on the distant treeline. "Fuckin' air support. That's a fuckin' joke. They dropped on our position, killed Leroy and Tony and blew me ten feet in the air. When I woke up, all I had on was my pants and boots. Pass me that canteen."

He slugged down what was left and pointed the aluminum jug at the paddy. "Our artillery came in like a shit storm and I started crawlin' around looking for cover or a hole, any place to hide."

A major from 1/5 approached us, still clean and tidy. "You guys from Foxtrot, right?"

"Why the fuck do you think we look like this... Sir." Robby didn't look up.

"Marine, I understand you had it rough but rest here for ten minutes then grab a rifle and ammo from that stack over there and report for assignment on the perimeter. They're still out there." He turned around and standing tall, returned to the center of the defensive position and safety.

"How the fuck would he know? Got any more water, Mac?"

I grabbed another canteen from the gear taken from our dead. "I'll find a couple of helmets and flak jackets too."

Robby sat still watching explosions light up the horizon. "It was dark by then. They must have dropped some two hundred pounders 'cause I found a crater four or five feet deep and ten foot across." He smiled and shook his head. "Right about then I promised God I would go to church if I ever made it back. So I rolled down inside. Only a direct hit was gonna get me.

"At first I thought it was a dead body. But when

an illumination round ignited overhead, I saw the guy was alive and just as fucked up as I was. Another barrage came in and we both started huggin' dirt clods."

I handed him a flak jacket, "Somebody from Second Platoon?"

Robby laughed. "He might have been from some second platoon in some fuckin' gook company."

"Jesus, Robby."

He was talking fast now, "Another round came in and blew dirt and hot shrapnel down in our hole. Think I went deaf for a while 'cause it got all silent. Didn't matter. I don't speak gook anyway." He picked up a piece of metal between his legs and threw it in the direction the major. "So we sat there staring at each other and covering up each time a gook rocket went off or somethin' from our side came in."

"Was he armed?

"Not even a knife. Didn't matter though 'cause everybody else was trying to kill us both. After a minute or two we kinda laid back and relaxed like we was the only two people left alive in the world."

Robby shook his head. "Sounds funny but for a moment,' he scooped up some dirt and let it sift down through his fingers, "I kinda felt like the war was over."

"What happened?"

"Well, the gooks must have pulled back 'cause the fighting faded away behind the ambush site and across the valley. It was dark but I could still see his face across the crater. A kid.

"He smiled and crawled up his side of our hole

and stuck his head up to listen. Then he turned around and nodded at me like it was OK, slid over the top and disappeared."

We sat for a while feeling the earth vibrate with the pounding across the paddy.

"It's weird, Mac. After what he and I went through out there, I felt alone, like part of me split off and was gone."

A staff sergeant dumped some gear in front of us. "You guys get it together and head over to that dug in position behind those boulders." We watched him walk away.

I handed an M14 and two ammo belts to Robby. Dried blood covered half the rifle stock.

He didn't move. "Mac, I don't think I can shoot anybody anymore."

"Are there cultures or tribes wherein individuals covet and protect their cherished memories and never speak of them for fear the retelling might diminish and steal the soul of the experience?"

Mac

NONG SON TRILOGY

History Revised

"Where the fuck you been for thirty years, Mac? "

A couple of truck loads of beer, half a dozen marriages and complications from combat wounds took its toll on my foxhole buddy. He looked fifteen years older than his fifty-five.

"Tell you the truth, Andy; I've been trying to forget about Vietnam. This is my first reunion. The hotel committee just happened to choose something close to my home."

"Stop feeling so uptight. I know what you did over there, so do these guys and you got respect from everyone here. I'll get you a drink. Relax."

I looked around the hospitality suite: happy faces, laughter, middle aged men hugging, hesitant newcomers dragged into small groups and drowned in the deep intimacy shared by survivors of the same trauma.

A photo display mounted on a sidewall caught my eye and I wandered over to check out the rows of youthful faces in a faraway land. Standing in the past, skinny young grunts leaned against bunkers and like playground warriors, posed with weapons and Marlboros.

Red and Chief, Sugar Bear and Smitty, Crazy Eddie and all the others, frozen in time, forever young. Their names? Where did they come from? How many lived, married, had kids, joined the Elks?

Inside a black and white snap shot with rippled edges a young Marine stood on a riverbank smoking a cigarette. A yellow Post-It marked with black marking pen identified "Rusty", in front of Nong Son Village.

"Here's a Jack Daniels and water, Mac. You need it. "

Andy turned and looked up at Rusty. "He got hit in Hue, didn't make it. Come on, Smitty's over there in his wheel chair and wants to talk to you."

I pointed at Rusty. "I was just thinking about living alone in the village up there. Remember? They sent me in to liaison with militia and collect Intel under the cover of teaching English. Living with those villagers changed my life. "

Andy stopped smiling. "Yeah. What a fuck job."

"What do you mean? And give me that drink."

Not known for his subtlety, the man I'd trusted with my life many times shook his head. "You dumb fuck, they sent you up there to die."

A swallow of Jack Daniels burned away part of the shock. Why would he come out with something like this? True, he loved his drink and drama but as a career Marine such a statement implicated his beloved Corps.

"Andy, come over here and sit down and lower

your voice."

We found two padded chairs in the corner overlooking Reno below. He flagged down a waiter. "Two more."

He leaned back and rubbed his stomach. "The VA put in some kind of material to replace necrotic muscle tissue. The itching drives me crazy."

I waited. He looked across at the photos. "A lot of those guys are dead because of the fuckup on Union II. We all knew it but you were the only one goin' around talkin' about it, even to the First Sergeant at Battalion. Remember?"

Union II. June 1, 1967. Twelve choppers lifted off with our guys. Six came back. Foxtrot Company used as bait. Foxtrot decimated. Too many body bags. Rows of empty cots. Me and Gunny Green the only survivors of the CP. Yes, I remembered.

I looked down at the whiskey in my glass. "I can't forget. I tried."

Andy sat up. "The hell you went through that night, I can't imagine. You must have been really messed up for a while 'cause you started makin' waves. Sayin' shit like, "Cowardice. Leaving our wounded. They wanted to get rid of you Mac, and not just transfer you because you would just keep talkin'. I gotta piss. Be right back."

He limped off and I stared at the photos across the room. Dozens dead, betrayed and buried under the god damned Code of Silence. Why had I come to the reunion? The only happy episode from the war, now in jeopardy: Nong Son Village…

Built by French missionaries and miners on the

banks of a brown water river, Nong Son smiled undisturbed like a post card from colonial days. Eight hundred souls from different levels of Vietnamese society lived in harmony and prosperity. Above them, an eighteen hundred foot hill held a company of Marines in three rings of defense. Mortars supplied fire support for ops in the valley.

Along the river stood rows of pastel colored stucco apartments once occupied by functionaires from the colonial mining operation. One small room with a rope sling bed and a hole on the floor for a toilet served as my home, office, and "intelligence" gathering center. In the corner on top of an ammo box stood my lifeline for rescue, a PRC 25 radio.

As the only American in the ville I might as well have been on Mars if the shit hit the fan. My qualifications? Two years of English Lit and four months of Vietnamese language school.

Andy's allegation began to make some kind of strange sense…

II
Teacher, Translator, Soldier, Spy
Fox Company HQ

"Looks like you survived another disaster, Corporal. You gónna run around and make trouble again?"

Fat, pale and a lifer, our new Ist Sergeant looked up at me from his desk in the safety of the command hooch. Another elementary school dropout from the South, his pressed uniform impressed no one. I could kill him later that night and no one would know. From the looks of the clerks around us, no one would care.

"Lt. Scuras got the word twelve hours before they overran us, Ist Sergeant."

"Just because you speak Gook, don't mean shit. He did the right thing and his report is now official." After a week in country behind a desk, he seemed to be an expert on combat operations.

Lt. Scuras and I were on delicate terms. A villager at great personal risk had warned me of VC infiltration before we got the hilltop got overrun at Nong Son. Would I inform Battalion? He offered to nominate me for Officer Candidate School. A bribe? A transfer? Guilt?

The desk jockey jabbed a folder up at me. "Battalion has an assignment here for you." He grinned and a second chin squeezed out under his first weak one.

I looked around at the typists and admin staff. Only La Barbera from Old Foxtrot still around, and he was a short timer. No back up, anywhere.

"Most of the guys from Union II and your fight on top of The Hill are no longer with us. As of today, this includes you. You're gonna go back up there; live in the ville and liaison with the militia. Good luck teachin' them English."

Fatso enjoyed power. A punishment in his mind, the transfer was salvation in mine. After seven months, I was an old timer and a threat to the new pecking order of non-commissioned officers. Foxtrot was full of replacements due to KIAs, wounded, disease, and rotations back home. Newbies could not be trusted and they saw those of us leftover from a string of losing battles as bad luck.

So the day came to load my rifle and new briefcase for a new mission: win the hearts and minds of English students and through them develop enough trust to gather intelligence in a remote village in the midst of a catastrophic civil war.

Two days later I climbed the metal steps up the side of a colonial coalmine to the abandoned offices and found the designated class room. The door stood ajar. The barrel of my rifle nudged it all the way open and poked into the silence.

Behind two folding conference tables sat twenty smiling men varying in age from twenty to eighty, erect and alert. The operational status of the mine hung in limbo. Before me, unemployed professional staff sat in Western clothes next to village elders in loose fitting traditional pajamas.

Now what?

I nodded and turned away to inventory the

classroom. A blackboard with no chalk, an empty bookshelf and a darkened window covered with coal dust made up the extent of teaching resource materials. Holy shit.

Outside and down the valley, explosions thumped as 80-mm mortar shells walked a trail of support for some poor patrol in trouble. Another day.

My students, all long time survivors, did not flinch and sat frozen like hungry disciples at The Last Vietnamese Supper. I was the only show in town. Most of them were older than me. What was I going to do?

I faced the blackboard and hung my rifle sling on the top corner of the frame. Lt. Scuras had given me his extra map case for lesson plans and materials. So with an empty briefcase I took a breath and turned slowly to face my platoon strength student body. Shit. I'd probably shot some of their cousins or brothers.

I saw not a single face. In a black hairy row, twenty heads of hair lined up like bowling balls at a bowling alley rack, all bowing in respect, not for me, but for the teacher.

Seven months of combat did not prepare me for this kind of fear. My legs shook. My brain collapsed. My heart raced. And just as in combat, when all is lost, I chose the only option: prayer.

A voice spoke within me. "Please God, if I ever do anything right, please make it now!"

I addressed the class. "Chao Cac Ong!" (Hello Group Male)

The hairy bowling balls straightened up in sync like a Marine Corps drill team and transformed into twenty smiling Vietnamese men.

"Chao Tai!" (Hello Teacher)

And thus began the first day of school and the happiest time of my life: a three month love affair with this small village, far away and a very long time ago…

III

Monsoon
Nong Son

"Can you hear me Mac? Nod your head. Good."

The sound of rain. A waterfall slid off the roof of the hut and poured down over cobblestones running to the Thu Bon River raging below. My fever burned hot and the medic from Echo Company shook his head, his distant voice fighting with the sound of the storm outside. "Mac, I can't get the temperature down. Only thing for that in my kit is aspirin. You gotta drink as much water as you can."

I said nothing. I couldn't.

"We need medivac but a no-fly order is in effect until this storm lets up. I gotta get back up the hill before dark or they might shoot me comin' in. Hate to leave you here alone."

Behind him, four or five of my students stood against a wall.

The security team leader stuck his helmet through the broken window. "Gotta go, Doc. Captain says now."

"See you tomorrow Mac." I felt someone pat my shoulder.

Motion. Whispers. Silence.

Cracks and patches in the ceiling plaster floated and danced above me in beautiful patterns sketching a map of my long journey from Los Angeles to the village of Nong Son.

"We help you, Tai." An elder pulled off my T shirt and fatigue pants. Naked, dizzy and near delirium

I could only lay exhausted, unable even to wonder if my shorts were clean.

Over the river, thunder boomed. Two of the younger men stood me up. "We help, Tai."

I leaned on them as they pulled and hugged me through the front doorway and into the monsoon. And there we stood. Under a torrent of water, two five foot human crutches supporting a six foot white ghost.

My temperature began to drop. Clarity returned and in a flash of lightening, I saw the smiling faces of my two saviors staring up at me. After fifteen minutes of Vietnamese hydrotherapy we returned to my room and old Quang dried me off before the three of them laid me back down. He covered me with a dry sheet, tucked me in and gently wiped my face.

He smiled. "Drink chai. Good." Hot tea stank of rotten roots and dark earth. He folded his arms across his chest and stood like a midget gunnery sergeant in black pajamas.

Quang turned down the lamp, gathered spectators and left the room. Yet I felt the presence of another, softer energy somewhere nearby. Gradually the ceiling stopped crawling and I began to dream…

…An elderly woman with white hair sat cross legged at the foot of my bed. In front of her, a charcoal brazier supported and heated a pot of tea. The dancing red glow of coals cast her shadow on the wall as she chanted and rubbed a string of wooden beads back and forth between wrinkled, ancient hands. I slept the sleep of the Dead.

A streak of sunlight splashed across the ceiling. Our monsoon had gone as quickly as it came and taken my fever with it. I felt renewed, born again, lighter in body and spirit. The after taste of tea from the night before filled my mouth accompanied by raging hunger.

Quang leaned against a post in the open doorway, smiling. He nodded in the direction of the far corner and I twisted around to look. The old woman from my dream smiled back as she sliced vegetables, making Pho soup.

Something strange and wonderful was happening to me. The tough combat veteran, now a helpless patient nine thousand miles from home had been won over by the hearts and minds of peasants in a remote Vietnamese village.

As a Marine, I was no good after that. The thought of shooting someone, anyone, belonged to a Self who no longer existed. I had been recruited and initiated into the human race. I now knew the real mission: to do as much good for the village as I could in what time I may have left to live.

Something had transformed me from within. Charged with purpose and meaning, I was full of energy. My days became alive and my body vibrated with urgency and purpose. I didn't want to go to sleep. I knew this new life, this new feeling could end at any moment. I didn't want to miss *anything*.

As the war around us intensified, I ate and slept in students' homes as they rotated me around like a circuit riding preacher. Returning to my own room in the mornings, footprints left evidence of midnight visitors. We never spoke of the danger. And in the Vietnamese way, only a gentle squeeze of my hand while inviting me to dinner sent the darker message that guerillas might visit that same night.

And so began the love affair of my life. Whatever intelligence, creativity and strength I was born with was called forth, valued, and embraced by those around me. Giving and receiving became one. My naïve suburban soul recognized something very precious and fragile and filled every moment of each day. It couldn't last.

The war continued around us and after three months I became a casualty, not of war but of hospitality. Each day, students manipulated and competed to bring me home for a meal. While flattered, I knew that my performance as the new oddity in town was much in demand. My repertoire of excruciating tonal accents, a few card tricks, songs and amusing cultural body language entertained and distracted families. After many meals of mysterious cuisine, I began to lose weight, energy and the ability to concentrate. River fever ended my stay and Doc from Echo Company called in a medivac.

On the flight to Tripler Hospital in Honolulu, I flirted with a flight attendant while a stream of brown liquid squirted down my leg and I waited to exit the plane last because of the brown spots on the seat of my pants. I stared out of the window as troops waved and yelled to ecstatic relatives waiting behind a temporary chain link fence.

In those days a portable stairway rolled up against the exit door and passengers departed onto the runway. Combat soldiers rushed to happy reunions waiting fifty yards away. Pow! An engine backfired in one of the luggage trucks under our plane.

Half of the disembarking troops dove onto the asphalt to take cover and in some sort of schizophrenic In Between Land; hands continued to wave to loved ones while bodies lay face down on the tarmac. Relatives froze like statues and for one brief moment caught a glimpse of the price paid by their sons and husbands.

Two months later, soft and civilian, the hospital released me and I returned to Phu Bai, Vietnam. With only three weeks left on my tour of duty, I drew new gear as Fox saddled up for Hue City and the rush to join with the enemy in the Tet New Year Offensive. Much has been written, filmed and documented of that battle and I prefer to bury my own memories in those accounts. In the midst of street fighting in the ancient capital, my tour expired.

I joined a few others on a truck back to Phu Bai and on to Da Nang for a flight to EL Toro Marine Corps Air Station, in California. Three days after landing, I exited through the front gates as a civilian with seven hundred bucks and no plan.

IINTELLEGENCE TRILOGY

I
No Escape
Bamako, Mali, Africa

He looked about thirty years older than me and a bit lonely. So I did my part and sat down next to him. "What's your program?

"Citrus tree propagation. You?"

"Water wells. Just got here."

"I leave soon for Niger River Valley region. How about a cup of coffee?"

"Not that instant crap please. The stuff gives me heart burn."

"I grew up in the Depression. Come on up for some real coffee, Cowboy coffee."

"Sounds good."

Our dormitory held a variety of Peace Corps Volunteers studying language and culture. My new friend from the Southern California orange groves lived on the top floor with a nice breeze. A hotplate soon glowed red and he sprinkled grounds on top of water boiling in one of the local aluminum pots. Smelled good.

"This your wife?" A couple of framed pictures stood side by side on top of the dresser.

"Yes, she passed away a few years ago." Only the sound of water bubbling and boiling.

"I'm sorry. This must be your son here? Looks like a Marine boot camp photo."

He came over, stood next to me. Silence.

I picked up the photo. "Good looking. Where's he stationed?"

"He was killed in Vietnam."

"Oh."

Shit. Six years after Nam and ten thousand miles deep into the Southern Sahara. Where did I have to go to get away? My neighbor was hurtin,' so as a former Marine, I did my part.

"What happened?"

"All I know is he was killed in the fall of 1967 on an operation called Hastings. No information, just a telegram.

But I knew. I knew exactly what happened. And again, I had done my part...

II
The Long Yesterday
Nong Son Village
1967

"Have some hot tea, Mr. Mac." He was much older than I and overweight, unusual for rural Vietnamese, even for a militia officer.

"Thank you Captain Thuy."

Nong Son's Catholic Church now held military and provincial administrative offices. Old Father Nguyen had fled to the safety of Da Nang long ago. The religion of French colonials no longer aligned commoners with powers struggling for control in their latest war. To enter and pray at Mass in an outlying region pinned a bull's eye on the back of any Catholic survivor from another time, another foreign occupier.

"How is your family, Captain Thuy? A new picture of your son perhaps?"

He smiled the smile of all proud fathers. "Yes. Here in drawer." The small black- and-white photo held a serious boy in a provincial school uniform.

"Thank you for bring Doctor Viti and help my wife."

In his culture, he was now indebted. I nodded and slurped some tea.

We spoke of family, food, and boredom. All the safe stuff. I waited and at the right moment, put my half-full cup on his desk. He nodded and poured more tea: a signal that staff had left for lunch in the village.

He looked over at the closed door then pushed a map of the local valley across his desk.

"They dig graves."

"Where?"

His chubby finger landed on a ville half way to An Hoa. "Here."

"How do you know?" Graves meant the enemy would stand and fight long enough to bury their dead. Very rare.

"My uncle have farm. They make him dig in trees. They come at night. Bring supplies."

Jesus. Two months of living alone in the ville and my first bit of intelligence. Had I won at least one heart and mind? If so, Thuy was taking a huge risk.

"Your name will not be spoken. Marines will send their own scouts to verify."

"Thank you, Mr. Mac. Now we must eat." A towel came off the tray on the corner of the desk, a feast from my favorite cook, his wife.

An hour later, I caught a ride up the hill to the command bunker of the Marine security company. The Captain listened to my story and turned to his battalion radioman in the corner.

"Call An Hoa and get me the Colonel. Good work, Mac. Maybe this will turn out to be something."

Village life flowed along and some pen-pal letters arrived from my old high school for my English students. As we read aloud in class, the soft "thump, thump" of heavy mortars traveled across the valley. Aircraft raced down the river at low altitude. Another operation launched.

Three days later, I ran into Andy as he got off the metal ferryboat on a resupply run from An Hoa.

"Hey Mac. How's the easy life?"

"Good. What's the news from Battalion?"

He dropped his pack on the riverbank and lit a cigarette. "Major fuckup as usual. Couple of days ago they sent out eight birds full of Echo Company on some op called Hastings. Seems they got info that the gooks were gonna stand and fight."

I got that bad feelin in my gut. "What happened?

"No recon. No prep, nothin. Scuttle butt says they flew right to the coordinates. Guys got shot as they jumped off the choppers. The gooks were there all right. Mortars came in. Too late."

He tossed his cigarette in to the river and watched it float down stream. "What's the matter, Mac?"

I couldn't speak. I felt hollow, empty of all hope for redemption. Never again would I pass information to anyone.

It was all insanity, meaningless.

III
Back in Bamako
Mali, Africa

I gently replaced the young Marine's photo on the dresser. Had I killed him? Did Thuy give me Intel to set up an ambush? I should have known command would fuck it up.

Time and ten thousand miles... no escape...

Part III
Symptoms

While both combatants and civilians often present lifelong symptoms it is possible through education and therapy to change responses when feelings and situations trigger "episodes". Although I worked for years with South Vietnamese Army veterans and their many challenges as refugees, I always provided services and seldom imagined that I too, needed help. Continuing employment in the social service industry focused on the client and postponed any need to look at my own symptoms; transience, fear of intimacy and the inability to imagine a future.

For the current generation of returning vets, how-to-heal manuals, movies, retreats, workshops, advocates, consultants, vet clinics, VA programs, online chat communities and media coverage are all part of the growing PTSD industry. It's not enough. Increased rates of suicide, homelessness, divorce and unemployment plague troops returning from the Middle East.

In the decades following my own tour of duty, I developed a pattern of coping. Successful moments of readjustment and routine normal life were followed by anxiety and flight. Predictable daily schedules triggered visceral memory of ambush and impending disaster. Episodes of transience, wandering and misadventures punctuated respectable positions in social service serving ex-cons, immigrants, refugees, low-income communities, third world countries, Native Americans and two tours with the Peace Corps.

I seldom looked at my own shit.

Survivors of trauma often recognize one another instinctually. This sort of mystical connection drove my employment choices and as a staff member of an agency, program, or institution, I believed I was guiding and helping PTSD survivors\. Boundaries got fuzzy. Emotionally disturbed vets and brown and yellow people were my community.... Just like the war.

The routine lives of suburban families began to hold some appeal and I arrived spontaneously on the doorstep of my oldest friend. As adult men who bonded during our teenage years we hugged and decades of estrangement dissolved. With a wife, five children, a big ranch-style home and a great career as a salesman he had created everything I walked away from: the American Dream.

A few nights later and alone in the back yard, he asked, "If I disappeared, will you stay around and help out with the kids?"

Shocked, I could only mutter, "Cancer?"

He shook his head and stared at the fire inside the big stainless steel barbecue and stabbed a hot dog.

"I can't stand all this anymore. I'm thinking of driving to the desert and disappearing."

Boy was I cured. He was fantasizing about my lifestyle and perceived freedom. I left the California suburb feeling much better about running around the planet and seeking out interesting experiences.

Sometimes, the experience finds us...

Time Bomb
Rohnert Park Vet Center

Dennis did his provocateur thing, "Why did you come to therapy today? You guys fought in the Good War. Everything was ok when you came back home."

The old man looked around our circle and shook his head. We could see a purple and silver yarmulke on the back of his head. "It wasn't my idea. The judge said I had to."

This was gonna be good. Other vets showed up now and then with court ordered participation in group therapy but this guy had white hair, was bent over with arthritis and maybe weighed a hundred thirty pounds

Our facilitator rattled his notes and in his compassionate counselor voice suggested, "Jacob, our process is to share just what incident brought you here to a group of fellow combat vets."

Show time. It's always awkward when the new guy tells strangers why he is fucked up. Jacob scouted the room to determine the threat level: (PTSD symptom 13). The ten of us were not only attentive but fucked up too. He seemed to feel a bit more comfortable and leaned back into an overstuffed easy chair. The rest of us sat on worn out donated couches, waiting. Medicated Joe stood by the open door, just in case he couldn't handle.

The old guy shrugged."Ten days ago I had the same bad dream I've been having for many years and woke up about three in the morning. This time it was really bad. So I got up, grabbed my robe and went out the back door to the tool shed in my back yard."

He stared at the US Army logo mounted on the wall above the coffee pot and doughnuts. "It was dark but the long handled sledge hammer was still leaning in the corner. I slung it over my shoulder and walked down the driveway onto my street."

Dennis elbowed me. His finely tuned hyper-vigilance could smell disaster coming.

Our intern had to do his psycho thing. "Please continue Jacob. We are all brothers in this circle and what's said here stays here."

Silence. Leave it to the professionals to break rhythm. You could hear a pin from a grenade drop.

His hands slid down and he gripped the shaft of his cane like a baseball bat. "I live in a quiet upper-middle class neighborhood. Everybody has a couple of cars and parks on the street in front of their houses." And just like asking someone to pass the salt, he said, "I smashed the front windshield of every German made car on the street."

"Jesus!"

"You gotta be fuckin' kidding."

"Way to go."

After we quieted down, Dennis stood up. "Must have felt fuckin' good." He walked over to Jacob and offered his hand." Welcome home, Brother."

Our counselor looked at his wrist watch. "What a wonderful gesture, Dennis. Now please take your seat and let's ask Jacob just why he felt it necessary to attack the private property of his neighbors."

"Could I get a glass of water?"

Three or four guys jumped up but Joe was closest to the water cooler. He brought over a paper cup and Jacob looked up at six and a half feet of grin cranked up on anti-depressants. "Thanks"

We all knew each other's story or in case worker lingo, 'psychic wound'. Dennis called group a pity party with a broken record but it's good to be around guys who went through the same shit and know what you're gonna say before you say it.

Jacob sipped from the Dixie cup, pulled out a handkerchief and blew his nose. "I got drafted and after training joined Patton's Third Army in France. The winter of '44 was tough but so were we. In the early spring of '45 we fought our way deeper into Germany, trying to beat the Russians to Berlin."

He started squeezing his handkerchief, maybe trying to pump up some courage. "By then I was radioman for Captain Keffer with the scout group of the 9th Armored Battalion. We got a message to turn south of Etter Mountain and I asked command for a landmark. Could I have some more water?"

Joe handed him another.

Behind Jacob on the wall, the second hand of the big round clock ticked heartbeats inside its black halo. "I can still hear the voice coming through static on the radio, the same voice that begins my dream almost every night, 'Buchenwald.'"

"Do you need a break, Jacob?"

"No. it's ok. I gotta get this out and done." He sat up a bit straighter and looked at each of us. "You guys are old enough. You've seen the photos of the inmates and their condition, the horror of the place.

"Well, the Captain knew I spoke Yiddish and some German so he grabbed me and we began walking through that nightmare. From out of one of the huts a naked skeleton crawled towards us on its hands and knees and whispered in Yiddish, "A sheynem dank, a sheynem dank." 'Thank you, thank you'.

"He collapsed and died with his hand around my ankle." Jacob watched shadows from an acacia tree outside the window sway across white floor tiles in the afternoon breeze. "I was nineteen."

He reached down and rubbed the back of his lower leg. "Patton showed up for a photo op and ordered the quartermaster group up along with our MASH unit. A few hours later, off we went to chase the bastards. I asked the Captain to send me back to my rifle platoon. He understood."

We all did.

Dennis asked again, "Jacob, why are you here?"

"Peace, god damn it, peace!" Embers from the same fire often raging within us flared up and for a moment, PFC Jacob Weinstein burned brightly. "Peace was declared a month later. The Nazis had not been punished enough. A few days after we set up permanent camp outside Berlin, I stole some warm clothes, a bunch of food and ammo and took off for the country side."

Joe limped into the circle and sat down. "They busted you for desertion?"

"No, murder." He touched his yarmulke and reassured, looked down at his hands. "From ambush, I killed every German soldier in uniform I could and still get away. The fourth body had a uniform my size without blood on it and time enough to change.

"After that, it was easy. In German, I called them over to have a smoke or bite to eat. I began to feel like an SS guard at Buchenwald carrying out the Final Solution. But this time," He stabbed the metal tip of his cane down hard on the white tile, "It was German soldiers exterminated, one at a time."

Tony, our spooky recon sniper, nodded. "I still want to go back to 'Nam as a tourist and pick off as many Commie politicians as I can. How many did you get?"

Jacob stared down the length of his cane as though sighting a rifle. "Dozens. Then the word got out and most Krauts in the area stopped wearing uniforms."

He smiled. "In training we learned camouflage and evasion. It took one of our Ranger platoons three weeks to catch me. Most of them shook my hand before they shipped me off to the psychiatric hospital set up outside Stuttgart."

His small body sank back into the forest print on faded cushions. After a moment, Jacob looked slowly around our perimeter, "Why are you here?"

PTSD QUINTET

I
Touch

Even now, this very moment, I feel it. A flash back? Hyper vigilance? Distrust? Fear of crowds? Need for isolation?

No.

Wouldn't it be great if it *were* just something mental? A pill, a drink or a doobie could fix it, at least for a little while. But on my deathbed, my old friend will whisper, "Still here."

We were animals back then, taking turns with the enemy: Predator. Hunted. Predator. Both sides miserable, exhausted, wet or hot, soaked or dehydrated, dirty, thin, and filthy. If we lived long enough we devolved and sank into the jungle of the sixth sense: an expanded aura constantly feeling and filtering the atmosphere around us for danger and death.

During our war hygiene was impossible for full-time combatants. Shaving, showers, shampooing, all these little pleasures ordinarily taken for granted were not only infrequent but inadequate. A swim in the Thu Bon River without soap and protected by heavily armed companions was the highlight of the month.

Our feet, armpits, and crotch targeted by insects, leeches, diseases and discomfort ached for treatment and relief. A powder or cream from Doc, our medic, helped for a few hours then slowly, inevitably, rice paddy, forest, or jungle once again worked its dark magic on foreign bodies.

As time passed a singular obsession developed: What one part of my body could be kept clean daily? What bit of sanitary sanity connecting me back home with The World could I defend and save from the overwhelming assault of The Bush?

The answer came roaring in on the weekly resupply chopper. Red and I were trading cans from C-rations at lunch when the H34 arrived at our outpost on Phu Loc.

Red's mother, warned of supply scavengers who "supported" us from safe areas, always sent two separate boxes. Support personnel soon learned to let one package slip through and kept the other one as payment. This time they must have been drinking or stoned. Red opened two identical packages.

"Hey, Mac." He spread out the latest treasures from Mom. "I got two manicure kits here. You want one."

I stopped chewing. "Let me see."

"You got two bags of chocolate, Red. What you gonna do with those?"

He stuffed both bags of Hershey Kisses into an empty ammo can.

"Eat this." He tossed a small leather sack and it landed in my C-rat box.

The zipper slid open easily. Inside, laid out and ready for inspection, a fingernail tool kit; half a dozen little items to trim, clean, and cut nails and cuticles. Shining brightly, a long slender blade sparkled in the tropical sun. I pushed it out of its collar and inspected it for sharpness. Why not?

I held the backs of my hands out in front of me and examined my fingers. The ten member squad stood at attention. Little black berets of dirt on top of each blank face.

Long accustomed to non intervention, the mud, red dirt, and rice paddy feces challenged me from under the middle fingernail. Black, thick and a quarter inch deep, a dark crescent moon helmet crowned the wrinkled finger below. Three months of neglect and fermentation had given birth to a formidable foe.

It took three days.

By the time we left the outpost and saddled up for rotation back to base camp, I was sure snipers would spot the sparkle off my shiny fingernails. Engineers swept the trail ahead for booby traps, and off we went. Everything felt the same as usual: hyper vigilance, free floating anxiety and paranoia. Yet this time something different vibrated.

My fingernails were sending me messages! "We're clean!" I must admit it was a bit distracting at first; ten little transmitters blasting away with a clear signal.

Yet the overall affect was reassuring. No matter what might happen in the chaos of combat, part of me transcended the filth of The Bush. I had control.

Over the next few weeks the messages became more subtle and differentiated. "Not clean. Getting dirty. Filthy. Pay attention!" So I did. We had an agreement and when neglected on my part, the signal grew in strength. Insomnia was the price. And so it went; monsoon, heat, dust and through-out the nights. I felt clean. Part of me was "not there." And somehow...

safe.

The messages have never stopped broadcasting. A moment ago I stopped typing to drag a nail file through dirt accumulated from gardening. Yes, I had to.

Twenty years after the war, my first therapist asked, "Does it make you think of Vietnam when your fingernails talk to you?"

I looked down at my old friends. "Doc, when they stop, it's time to commit me."

II
Sight

"Hey. These handcuffs are cutting into my wrists."

"Sorry, they're the new plastic ones. Sit tight back there. We're almost to the county jail."

The back seat of the Sheriff's patrol car was not built for comfort. Thick transparent seat covers installed for queasy drunks provided little cushion, so I sat up straight to take the pressure off my hands, locked behind me.

The deputy was a decent sort. "Have you ever received psychiatric treatment or been hospitalized for mental problems? Don't lie to me. I'm running a background check on you right now. You seem like a reasonable guy. How'd you ever get into a mess like this?"

I leaned back and thought for a second, How did this happen...?

Oh yeah. The Viet Cong. It was their fault, still extracting revenge and reparation after thirty five years. In vivid flashback, I saw sand-bag bunkers and the metal airstrip at An Hoa. Gunny Jones had us standing tall out in front of Fox Company hooches.

"OK you Shitbirds, you're issued one standard packet of Rit Dye, color: Forest Green. At 1800, you will be back here in formation with your skivvies: displayed, dry, and dyed fuckin' green! And you all know why! Some fuckin' retard general in Da Nang had another brilliant fuckin' idea."

I tried not to look at Rabbi, who was scratching his butt. Wounds itched when healing, and Rabinowitz just got back from the infirmary after a week of lying on his stomach. A sniper got him as 2nd Platoon took a break on a sweep down by the river.

Rabbi wandered off, squatted down to crap in the rice paddy just like a villager, and over his shoulder yelled, "This kosher manure will help out big time."

Young green plants blended with his dirty green fatigues and helmet. Everything went as planned until he dropped trou. Hanging out there for every sniper in Vietnam to see was a big white bull's eye in the field of green. Cowboy had to crawl out and drag him back while the platoon fired randomly into the distant tree line.

Rabbi had joined the growing number of ass wounded grunts, a statistic passed up to decision makers at the Imperial Hotel in Da Nang, no doubt during happy hour.

The following day and wearing newly dyed

underwear we saddled up with sixty pounds of gear and left base camp for the long walk to Nong Son Hill. Hot and humid, we were soaked in sweat before losing sight of perimeter at An Hoa.

Two hours later, we crowded onto a metal ferryboat and relaxed for a few minutes before the uphill hike to fan out and assume security positions. We stared in envy as supply truck drivers began the climb up the fifteen hundred foot outpost.

Cowboy, Rabbi, Doc, and I found our small bunker on the second ring of defense about eight hundred feet above the river. We unloaded gear. Cowboy began to scratch. "Jesus. I got bugs or sumpin, Doc."

"Take off your flak jacket and shirt. I'll have a look."

Sunlight still splashed across the top half of the hill so the three of us gathered around to have a look. At first, it looked like Cowboy wore two T-shirts. He took off the first one but his upper body was still green. Warm sweat had washed the cheap dye out of cheap cotton and into his skin.

"Pull your pants and shorts down, Cowboy."

He did.

Rabbi laughed. "Holy Shit. It's the Incredible Hulk! Except for your dick, Cowboy."

"Fuck you. Take your shirt off."

He did.

We did.

Four green grunts.

Doc pointed at my radio. "Mac, call the CP. Then get the infirmary on Battalion Net. If Cowboy is allergic, others will be."

Cowboy smiled and stopped scratching. "Guess I gotta go to China Beach for quarantine, huh Doc? I might be contagious."

Rabbi pulled up his pants. "Probably poisoned Viet Cong dye. Your dick's gonna fall off."

"Yours is already gone, Pee Wee."

Well, between Rabbi getting shot in the ass for exposing Bulls Eye Brand Boxer Shorts and a dozen green grunts with allergic reactions on their private parts, most of us stopped wearing underwear of any kind. Eventually the dye wore off… but not the paranoia.

Yes, I confess: I don't wear underwear and had lunch at a sunny outdoor café in my swimsuit where my balls must have slipped out. Some frustrated housewife called the cops, and now I'm on the way to jail in this police cruiser for indecent exposure.

No, the VC didn't get me. But they're still out there… waiting.

III & IV
Taste and Smell

He pushed the half empty bottle of Colonel Taylor across the table.

"Join me?"

Outside in the backyard the party raged on. As usual, I had drifted away seeking sanctuary, this time into a small kitchen.

He nodded at an open dishwasher where a

column of glasses stood at attention, bottoms up. I grabbed one and sat down across from him. Older by a dozen years, he stared at me from someplace far off and in that moment, I knew him.

"Thanks." I poured a bit of whiskey into a tumbler and leaned back. The well used chair under me protested and squeaked a note in synch with the boom box outside.

"Can't take it either?" He slid his empty glass my way and I grabbed the jug by the neck. The Colonel bowed in a salute. Mission accomplished.

I took a sip and said it. "Army?"

"Korea." He saw who I was…. "You?"

I nodded. "Marines. Vietnam."

Our shared past, different but the same, rose up and held us both. We sat there looking across a suburban kitchen table into a mirror.

He raised his shot glass in a toast. "Better dead than Red."

We laughed, and the old familiar darkness retreated.

"Some chow over there on the counter. Like Vietnamese food?"

"No. That smell of fermented fish sauce really gets to me."

"Why?"

I turned around and scouted the back door and deck outside. No civilians. The nightly fog began to creep over the ridge and down into Mill Valley from Stinson Beach.

"Well, villagers and the Cong used that sauce on everything they ate out there in the boonies, probably to kill bugs. Fermentation for three days brewed up quite a stink. They called it, 'nuoc mam', means fish water."

"Sounds like Korean Kim Chee."

"It wasn't hot like that. It just reeked. Anyways, nights in the jungle were so dark we couldn't see shit, might as well had our eyes closed. We'd be laying out on ambush, all in a row and side by side. Our senses became alive, mostly hearing and smelling. I guess blind people must feel that way every day."

He placed his glass down on the table without a sound. "Go on."

"The forest got so hot and humid at night we began to sort out different scents and sounds, kinda like dogs. You know what I'm talking about."

"Yes...."

"Pitch black, no sounds, no forward recon post to warn us... just laying there in some kinda blind man's Hell, waiting. Everybody got nervous out there at night; us, them, monkeys, everybody. So plus the heat we sweat that nervous sweat. There's a difference, a stronger smell.

"Then it would happen, just a whiff at first... nuoc mam. That damn sauce. They were crawlin up on our position, just as scared as us and sweatin out that fermented shit. Soon as it got stronger we would fire our weapons in the direction of the smell and then duck."

He sniffed a few times and raised his arms. "Don't shoot, Brother! There's some Pizza over there on top of the stove."

Our laughter attracted a couple smoking a joint

in the bushes, and the girl poked her head across the threshold into our space. "What's going on in here?"

My new friend stared at me and shook his head. Silence sent her back outside, searching for some other distraction.

He looked down into the empty shot glass. "Back in Korea we had something like that goin' on. Part of the year, ground fog was so thick you could see maybe ten foot in front of you, even during the day. We were trying to hold onto some shit ground and spent a lot of time in trenches and foxholes. I haven't thought of this for a long time. Give me the last of that rye."

The amber liquid swirled around for a moment, then became still, clear.

"In the spring, fog was actually warm, a nice blanket smothering hills all around us, perfect cover for an attack... Wait. That's all we did. Wait. We knew they were coming. It was just a question of when."

He reached across to his other hand and rubbed the stump of a missing finger. "Just like you guys, all we could do was lie there and hope for some kinda warning. And like you, we smelled something that gave them away. When we got a whiff, we opened up too."

"Kim Chee?"

"No. Something much stronger. You see, when the Chinese came down across the border they brought their herbs and shit in a medicine pouch. Every gook had one tied on his belt. Every day they ate garlic as a cure-all. Garlic. Man, I still hate that shit."

"Jesus. They ever figure it out?"

"No. Maybe they thought we had motion detectors or something. But after a while I guess they ran out of the stuff, cause we went back to just being blind in the fog."

We sat there in silence for a while, each lost in our own foggy memories. Then it happened. We looked across the table of empty glasses, remembering.

In the same instant, a light bulb went off, not overhead on the kitchen ceiling but in our heads. As though finding a new piece in a puzzle thought solved decades ago, we smiled, "What did they smell from us?"

It didn't take long. "Shaving lotion!"

He laughed so hard his stomach jarred the table knocking Colonel Taylor over, sending him rolling toward the edge. I stood him back up. Our grins filled the room.

"How did your guys do it in 'Nam? Our Southern boys would drink anything with alcohol; liquid shoe polish, brake fluid, mostly shaving lotion. They'd stand a loaf of rough gook bread on end and pour the stuff down through it. Hillbilly Filtration, they called it."

"In 'Nam we had guys called The Aqua Velva Squad." I don't think they filtered anything, just sucked down four ounces of that 40 proof blue shit. On patrol, we made them walk rear because we could smell them up front ahead of us."

And like tripping a booby trap we stared at each other in the blazing glory of discovery. How many of our guys had triggered an ambush while stinking from a cocktail of Old Spice?

Colonel Taylor was dead. No replacement stood tall. It wasn't gonna get better than this and we both knew   it.

"Time for me to leave, Jarhead. I'm gonna collect my lady and go back over the bridge. Thank you, Brother."

"You too. Every time I have garlic I'll think of tonight. What do you think? Should we advise our generals in Iraq about shaving lotion?"

He turned around in the doorway and looked down at the recently retired Colonel Taylor and our empty glasses.

"Fuck it. It all evens out."

V
Sound

Someone yanked on my tee shirt. "Daddy, let's go back to the swings."

There it was again, that far away sound. I could almost figure it out.

"Come on Daddy, why are you staring?

Yes, that was it. A rope was blowing in the wind and slapping on a metal flagpole. But where? Nothing in sight across the hundred meters of the exposed grassy knoll in front of us Part of me stood somewhere else... listening for something else.

"Can't you hear it, Honey?"

"What Daddy?'

A leaf tumbled in the wind and I heard each

little summersault whisper across the grass. On the side of the field, bamboo planted to shield neighbors from the playground, scratched in the breeze. Where was I?

She screamed. "They're coming!"

I reached for something, something no longer there.

"Mommy!"

She picked up our daughter and saw my hand grasping for an invisible weapon no longer there. "Let's go home. I'll drive. You take the baby."

"I'm OK."

She tried to smile. "It takes time."

Six blocks down the street we passed an elementary school with its flag flying at half mast. The rope, too tight and driven by the wind, slapped against the metal pole.

She was crying now. "Why did they have to shoot King?"

My daughter patted her shoulder. "It's OK, Mommy.

I thought of Terry King in Echo Company and as we turned the corner, I said to the windshield, "It's too tight."

Somewhere, someone agreed. "I know."

Part IV
First Steps Home

So I set out again. Lost and adrift, I knew that while civilians around me embraced the same world I had left there was no place in it for me. The consciousness, aspirations and dreams of my childhood friends no longer meant anything.

Life on the road matched the familiar pattern of a patrol and temporary companions. Academic semesters and employment contracts reflected the timeline of a tour of duty: twelve months. Intimacy and fear of loss resulted in abandonment as I moved on. These well know symptoms of PTSD are now easily found on an Internet search. But in 1969 symptoms shaped and drove my daily life. It was 'normal'.

And like a good Marine, there was one last mission...

"Now, you will not swell the rout
Of lads who wore their welcome out,
Runners whom renown outran
And the name died before the man."

To an Athlete Dying Young
A.E. Houseman

Heart Song
Bellaire, Texas

"Come on, Mac. Put your shit in your bag and we'll drive you over there. His family knows you're coming and they're waiting."

Even though shot in the ass the previous year, Ron still played Boy Scout with what passed for *joie de vivre* in Texas. Jimmie smiled his big country-boy smile content with his traditional role as Sidekick. They scouted the hotel room for my clothing and personal items. Soon a small pile grew on the top of the bed.

"Grab his bag, Jimmie. It's in the closet."

I still wasn't ready after a long train ride across the Southwest. I needed time; time to figure out what I was going to say to Mike's folks. Instead of going directly to their home, I had rented a room downtown and called some Marine Corps pals in Houston.

While I was a decorated Marine, multilingual world traveler and held a PhD in charming bullshit, I was terrified. Somewhere between fulfilling a promise to the parents of a deceased friend and my talent for high drama I was about to navigate new territory without a compass or map.

"OK, Ron. I'll go, but I need a drink." Both Texans smiled.

The three of us had studied and drank our way through the Defense Language Institute in Monterey, California. We stumbled through the Vietnamese program and somehow wound up together in the same battalion in 'Nam.

Now here we were a year after our tours in our prime, full of hormones in Houston, Texas and heading for the hotel bar. Eleven thousand miles from Vietnam and in civilian clothes we entered the elevator on yet another patrol.

By midnight, liquid courage flowed through me and I recited a poem by Ferlinghetti, pissing off every Catholic in hearing distance. Something about, "Jesus, Being all hung up...."

Ron had heard it all before. "OK, Mac, enough. Jimmie and I have to work tomorrow. Your bag is in the car. Let's go."

In the back seat, I watched skyscrapers dissolve into suburbia as we turned from the boulevard onto a residential street. Ron stopped his Valiant and turned the engine off. "Here it is. The lights are still on so just go on up and knock on the door."

I leaned forward between the two of them. "Aren't you coming in with me?"

Jimmie shook his head. "Damn it, Mac. They ain't the Viet Cong you know. Now go do it."

As I walked up the path to the house, Ron and Jimmie watched to make sure I did my duty and that someone answered the doorbell.

I dropped my bag on the porch, stared at a little white button and after a minute pushed it. Four notes belled softly inside, chairs scraped, voices, then footsteps. The doorknob turned. My heart drummed loudly and I stood like a frozen statue under the porch light. The door swung open.

"Mac!"

And there they were. Mike's parents. Just as I'd imagined. They hugged, kissed and dragged me inside. My anxiety dissolved in a frontal assault of love and celebration. I turned around to see Ron and Jimmie nodding and smiling. The Valiant pulled away from the curb, their mission accomplished.

A year of correspondence with Mike's mother had sketched a family portrait of wholesome Americana devastated by the loss of their beloved son. Now a little overdue perhaps, a friend had traveled to their home to help replace a two year old, yellowing telegram.

In the following week I lived an entire lifetime. Mike's dad and I stayed up nights until neighborhood dogs barked at the paperboy in the morning. As he was a survivor of the Battle of the Bulge in WWII, we found common ground and language.

Loquacious, capable and dynamic, Mrs. Driscoll played tour guide as we attended church, visited Mike's high school, turned the pages of family albums and after a few days stood before her son's grave.

"Do you like his epitaph, Mac?"

I read the carving on the tombstone. 'Corporal Victor Michael Driscoll, 1947-1967, USMC,

Vietnam.'

"Yes. It's fine."

But Mike was not a typical Marine. Sensitive, articulate and kind, he seemed miscast in the violence of combat. He carried an aura of fatalism and those of us with many months of experience sensed that he would not survive.

I slept in his old room and was encouraged to make it my own. Inside an old wooden trunk I found a huge stack of notebooks filled with poetry written by Mike. I read it all. Romantic and idealistic, he wrote on the theme of dying bravely and young. Then I understood: a self fulfilling prophecy. Perhaps he got what he wanted.

Ron fixed me up with a great gal, Jimmie gave me his old car, a friend of Mr. Driscoll offered me a job and my friendship with Mike's fourteen-year-old brother flourished and deepened. Bellaire, Texas gave me the homecoming I had never received in my own community. Everything was great. It was all so dreamlike yet uncomfortable.

I began to feel as though I might become a replacement for Mike. And I knew it was time to go.

The Driscolls understood. They hugged me and agreed that everything had happened too fast and I needed to leave and "find myself". As she poured more coffee, Mrs. Driscoll smiled at her son's academic awards mounted on the family-room wall.

The back door popped open and Mike's brother tossed his baseball mitt on top of the TV. "What's up?"

Mrs. Driscoll held my gaze and nodded.

What could I possibly say? "How was practice? Let's go talk in the bedroom."

For a week he had been happy to talk of grownup stuff and share secrets his parents might have found uncomfortable. He lost his big brother, and now I was about to leave.

In Mike's room we stood in front of the window and stared out at the backyard where two brothers had wrestled, played catch, told secrets and planned their futures.

I looked down at him and confessed, "It's time for me to leave here. I thought I was coming to help you guys and I'm the one who got all the good stuff."

He looked back again outside at the rusty swing set. "You are my brother now."

Oh shit. The last thing I wanted to happen. Would he follow Mike and I, enlist and come home lost and confused or not at all?

I struggled. He felt my hesitation.

His hand felt warm on my arm and like an older brother he looked at me and said, "It's OK, Mac. I love you." His hand fell away. "But I don't wanna be like you."

That night, the Greyhound Bus agent sold me a ticket for Bloomington, Indiana. L.T. Brown from our infantry training regiment said he had a bedroom for rent and a job at the pizza parlor in town.

Cpl. Driscoll

The soon to die
Parade in review,
Replacements for
The already dead.

We, the almost dead
Many times,
Search for the mark
Of the Beast

Among these
Clean-clothed
Baby-faced,
Well fed
Bodies

Assembled
In formation,
Their fate
Already written
In ancient script...

Known only by us:
The almost dead.
The plot, a mystery,
The timing, soon.
Death's name signed
On a contract
Made long ago.

These Chosen
Stand with one boot
In the grave.
And through grace,
Are blind.

Yet
We are mute.
To call out, to interfere-
The Beast may turn
His gaze…
Our way.

Our own time
will come.
Our contract
With this dark shadow
Is already…

Signed.
Mac

"It is a good thing to escape from death,
But it is not great pleasure
To bring death to a friend."

Sophocles

Shakespeare Speaks
Sonoma State University, CA

"Today, we finish the last scene in Julius Caesar. Over the weekend read 'Hamlet' and we will begin discussion on thematic parallels within the two plays during Tuesday's class."

About a dozen of us sat in a circle, a circle designed to lubricate intimacy and to create an audience for those of us assigned to read aloud. It was a summer class, the last one available and I had signed up to qualify for a stipend offered by the GI Bill. It seemed Shakespeare was not highly regarded by the administration for our classroom had no windows. It was hot, just like the battlefield scene we were about to review.

I was older than the others by a dozen years, enrolled in my fifth university, postponing any effort to re-enter mainstream America and beginning not to care. Like other citadels of learning, we had a base with many buildings, instructors to train us, specialty schools, comrades, and graduation for successful study. Of course, we were all just warm bodies replacing the casualties, dropouts, graduates, and no-shows. Without student fodder there would be no tenure for career lifers. Shakespeare helped pay the rent for both the professor and me.

Dorothy Overly was a tough broad, around fifty five, kinda ugly and wide. Yet our professor was full of energy and dramatic expression. She reminded me of the middle-aged buck sergeant from Alabama who taught a heavy weapons class at Camp Pendleton. We would gratefully remember the lessons he forced into us.

Overly sat under the clock at the top of our circle, staring at each of us in turn, daring us not to care. "Understanding what the classics have to offer is truly a gift from antiquity, a past with characters who have confronted the slings and arrows of life's misfortune. We here must face many of the same misfortunes in the course of living out our own life's script. Some of us already have."

Why was she looking at me?

She stood. "Actually feeling the charaters' exquisitely chronicled lives is a blessing that connects us to humankind and to our own soul. Observing and applying these universal lessons can more fully integrate our own personal past and help us to face the yet unknown challenges to come. But this, my fellow travelers, requires feeling."

She took her seat between two students with complexion challenges and opened her purse. Pulling out a tissue box, she set it in front of her on the desk. A pack of Camels peeked out from the still open handbag.

"Check today's guideline and find the part assigned to you. Let us take ten minutes and silently read scene five. Rumor has it that we all have hearts and souls. Some of you may even have experience.

Use these. Try to match your emotions to the character's situation, and imagine being him, being there, long ago."

Then sitting in her chair, staring at nothing, Dorothy Overly went away. Not day dreaming but really gone. I had seen it in combat many times. Maybe she was a Buddhist or something or just burned out on students taking her classes to accumulate credits. Or maybe she had at one time left her books, her dead authors and lived a life Shakespeare might have written.

Scanning the assignment, I found my new identity: Brutus, a good guy but he got drafted and joined the wrong cause: frag Caesar. Our similarity ended there. He had his own legion. I carried a rifle and a pack. Up to now, Julius Caesar had accurately portrayed the classical functions of all politicians and officer corps: ambition.

So I picked up my book and flipped through to the last act. Generals were whining and arguing about dead Caesar and what to do. Meanwhile, honest legionnaires whose names were never recorded waited on the field to die. Shakespeare sure got that part right. Maybe he served in the military. I kept reading.

The battle began. It was all very familiar stuff: poor Intel, lousy communications, tactical blunders; the usual chaos. My guy Brutus moved too fast and the shit started rolling down hill. His side lost and nobody wanted to be taken prisoner, just like in the Nam. About to be overrun, one of the generals, Cassius, committed suicide. Good thing he did it right. The Romans did not have guns and after using a knife or sword on themselves, half the time they woke up in a tent with the enemy smiling down at them. Not good. I kept reading.

Act Five. Scene Five. Julius Caesar
The armies of Mark Anthony and Octavius have defeated the legions commanded by the conspirators who assassinated Caesar. Capture is worse than death.
Brutus to Strato:
Thou art a fellow of good respect thy life hath some smatch of honor in it. Hold then my sword, and turn away thy face while I do run upon it. Wilt thou Strato?   W
Strato:
Give me your hand first. Fare you well my lord.
Brutus.
Farewell, good Strato. Caesar, now be still. I killed not thee with half so good a will. *Dies.*

A soldier helping his friend to die? A mutual obligation? An act of love? I started feeling funny, kinda frozen like. In those days, I couldn't sleep, and sometimes I got a little disjointed, but this was just a class in a suburban school, just a book.

Tropical perfume from the student next to me floated over my desk, her pungent plumeria blending with my nervous sweat. I looked around and the circle of desks faded into fog from the Central Highlands. Underneath me, brown linoleum tile transformed into rice paddy dirt. And scattered like rag dolls, a ring of bodies rose up out of the past. I heard Okie's voice. But this time, I was awake.

Final Scene. Operation Union II

Foxtrot Company is about to be overrun by superior forces of the North Vietnamese Army. Okie has been gut shot.

Okie to Mac:

Do it, Mac! Please! You stay, you die!

Mac.

Jesus Okie. Jesus!

Okie.

I'm dead any way. Don't let em get me!

The enemy approaches, torturing, executing wounded on the field. Mac to Okie, crying.

Goodbye Okie.

Okie.

Thank you.   *Mac kills Okie and flees.*

"Wake up Mr. MacKinnon. Page 82, line 23 if you please." She was staring at me from across the circle, across time. Somehow I got through the reading and back home to the trailer court. And then the strangest thing of all happened: I slept through the night for the first time in years.

At the end of the semester our professor hosted a class party at her town house a few miles from the university, a civilized affair. Well-read undergrads tried to impress each other and our much loved mentor. Later in the evening, my hostess and I found ourselves alone at the snack table.

She smiled her big toothed smile and sipped from a tumbler of Irish whiskey. A gold band suggested a husband but there was no other evidence in the living area or adjoining rooms.

She gave me The Look. "Are you Mac or Brent?"

I kept chewing the miniature quiche knowing this was a moment not to hide behind a camouflage of humor. "I don't know, Dorothy."

"Come with me." She took my hand and we wove our way through the conversations, flirtations, and wannabe intellectuals. She closed the den door behind us, crossed over to the desk and opened the top drawer. An old black and white photo in a tarnished silver frame floated on a sea of letters written in a masculine hand.

She drained her glass and smiled. "Meet my husband."

Dorothy Overly put her arm around my waist. A Marine in combat fatigues and parka sitting on snow covered sandbags smiled up at us from the desk. You could tell: he was one of the rare ones thriving in the most difficult of circumstances, his spirit soaring, senses electric, at home with his comrades.

"This is my Charlie. He was killed at the Chosin Reservoir twenty-five years ago."

She became very still and I knew then the place she visited in these moments. I looked up. Marine memorabilia hanging on the opposite wall began to blur and I felt the presence of bare Korean hills in winter, the rainforest of Vietnam and the dusty plains outside of Rome.

"He was always just Charlie, wherever he was. That's the secret, my friend."

She sighed, straightened up, and put Charlie

back in that special place where she kept him.
"Come on. I need a drink. And, Mac?"
"Yes, Dorothy?"
"Will Shakespeare was there with you."

Testimony
Fredonia, New York

The day finally arrived when faculty advisors in the Linguistics Department asked me to choose a topic for the Master's thesis. What to do? Maybe some coffee and pie at the local restaurant would lubricate my imagination.

Sitting at the counter, I stared at fat round pies under glass. Indecision seemed to be the flavor of the day and I couldn't decide between apple and rhubarb, cold or hot, alamode or not.

The white jacket of a bus boy stopped in front of me. "Wata ?"

And there holding a tray of water glasses, stood my thesis: a Vietnamese refugee.

Over the next months, Vinh Lu came to my apartment three nights a week on his way home. He was thrilled that an American on the distant planet of Upstate New York had once visited his own land, spoke his language and both of us – survivors of the same war.

So I began tape recording interviews, making language acquisition notes for my thesis and when trust found its way into his heart, I asked Vinh to tell me of his village life in Vietnam. He had just been relocated to the US from a refugee camp in the Philippines and true to Vietnamese character he poured out his memories in a flood of emotion.

During our last week together he brought his diary to my home and with the help of his English, my Vietnamese and a bi-lingual dictionary we struggled to translate excerpts at random. I learned that like many of the Marines in my infantry, unit Vinh had been drafted into military service.

One evening after completing the translation a difficult passage, I laid the diary down on the kitchen table and looked across at my savior. Our wrinkled green table cloth seemed to ripple in a wind from another time, another place. The same fertile rice paddy in my reoccurring dream lay between us as it once had in the past...

Opposite me sat a fellow warrior, my new friend and a Viet Cong guerilla.

The Diary of Vinh Lu

Song Vau Village
February 12, 1980

They are all dead now, all except me.

My brother Binh died yesterday here in our village holding a rake out in front of him like the rifle he once carried so well. His last target was the resident ghost of an enemy who over the years had become his friend. Nights around the fire, Binh laughed and told us the dead American boy waited for him in the next life. They are together now; gone to that place we all must one day visit.

The war had made Binh unafraid. In those rare moments when he did not smile, he stared into the darkness over the river and provoked the shadow world with his whispers, "We shall meet soon."

Only in this did he move from the common heart we all shared in our village. And while we feared the many phantoms around us, we forgave Binh a

92

thousand times for he was ever our friend, our living spirit and the best among us. We loved him like no other.

Our land is full of ghosts, wandering souls who died violently, ripped from their bodies and their unfinished lives. Confused and with no living family to honor them, no altar where they receive veneration and nourishment, they cannot guide new generations through this troubled land. Their fate is to wander, wander without purpose, without end.

A poet to the last, Binh fell face down in the season's harvest, his thin body pushing up a gentle fog of rice dust. Pierced and illuminated by the morning sun, the mist wrapped him in a shining shroud. I watched his last breath flow silently out his scarred body without complaint and become one with the chi of our village. In tender caress, pollen settled upon him, blessing his last moment.

This small cloud was his only cremation. We no longer had wood to coffin our dead. Profiteers stripped our valley of hardwood a decade after the War of Liberation against the Americans. Our young people care nothing for the past know almost nothing of history, and the always-corrupt Southerners exploit our future as they ape the lifestyle of the foreigners who almost destroyed us. What did we really win? The poor remain poor. It seems only the face of the tax collector changes.

Binh and I once felt the excitement of youth. Are all young men so easily seduced by promises of a glorious cause? Did the American boy Binh had killed believe the propaganda in his own village? I remember when the political officer first came to us and began the classes, our first of many. Most of all I remember his announcement that soon, the men of my village must volunteer.

Diary Entry
Son Vau Village
April 9, 1963

All the men of our village sat on the ground in obedient rows, legs crossed with calloused, anxious hands folded in our laps. Why were we not in the fields? Facing us, six armed NVA soldiers stood side by side and in front of them, a small tidy man in a Northern uniform.

He did not smile. "After a hundred years our victorious national forces expelled the French, their imperialist occupation and their hired mercenaries, The Legion.

"Peace and reunification of our country seemed near. Our hearts joyful and full of gratitude but in a last dishonorable act, the French armed and anointed their Catholic puppets. Branding our beloved national leader and our People's Army as communist they looted the last of our treasury and sailed away.

He nodded towards the border. "True, we now accept help from the Northern Dragon. When no one else steps forward, then a bargain must be struck. The cost of business with Beijing is always high. We will deal with them in the season of reckoning. Now in their fear, the Southerners welcome yet another devil from the West. "

Binh could talk without moving his lips, and

just as in our lower form school days, his goal was to cause me to laugh so that I might reap a rich harvest of consequence. It was a game we played. I owe him much for this gift. He forced me to think and speak quickly, early training for my career was an interrogator.

My brother's whisper mimicked the nasal pinch of the northern official.

"And as soon as Comrade Dwarf removes the sugar cane stalk from up his ass, we can plant it and see what the harvest will really be."

I managed to choke down a giggle with a spasm of gagging. Binh pounded me on my back and apologized to our guest.

"A childhood affliction, Comrade. He may not be fit for a Home Defense Team."

Healed instantly by the political officer's silence, I sat at attention, put on my respectful face and waited.

"Your name, Afflicted One?"

"Vinh Lu, sir."

"Our first team assignment will assist you in regaining your health and through this, appropriate behavior. You will assume command of daily drills on the soccer field. Consider this an opportunity."

"Yes Comrade."

"May I assume that your partner in this little charade is your twin?"

"Yes Comrade."

"His privilege is to write daily evaluations of your performance as drill instructor."

Binh smiled and saluted. "Yes Comrade!"

Our instructor turned his narrow shoulders to us and pointed to a map of Quang Tri Province nailed on a tree. Few of us had ever visited the locations drawn on the map. Why would we? Our land, our animals and the Thu Bon River sustained, nurtured and healed us when sick. All this was soon to change.

I squirmed and mumbled. "What's a drill?"

Diary Excerpt
February 12, 1980
Son Vau Village

Binh is gone now. Across from me, his chair sits empty and the chessboard calls out, aching to come alive like a rice paddy in dry season. Our game waits for troops to move back and forth, striking now from a distance, now close enough to touch the enemy and always manipulated by hands from above.

Sometimes when the wind blows down from the mountain, I can still hear our voices as we played at war....

Diary Entry
February 1, 1976
Son Vau Village

I opened with King's pawn and asked my opponent, "Do you think the Americans honor their ancestors as we do?"

Binh sat across from me, our chessboard serving as venue for yet another discussion.

"Their dead tell us stories."

He stared at his hands and at their twin shadows cast down upon red earth behind my house. The hand with the missing two fingers dug into his vest pocket.

"Why do I still carry this?" He slid a faded photograph across the chessboard.

The past rushed over our soldiers on the board and pulled us back into the time of suffering. In the picture, an old couple stands on a porch somewhere in America. They are waving at their loved one as they have for seven years and always will until the photo finally fades and like their beloved family member, they too disappear.

Binh rubbed the stumps above his knuckles and moved his knight forward into jeopardy.

"He took my fingers and I took his life. Why does my hand itch only when I think of him?"

"Binh, you itch for you know the young peasants they sent here to fight were like us, pawns in the hands of greater players in a game we could not imagine. They died as we died, calling out to mothers or sweethearts and clutching photos not of leaders but of family." Camouflaged by two pawns my bishop slid into position.

"Perhaps you are right, Vinh. I still see him in my dreams. A child, really."

He looked down at the board, saw the danger, and asked quietly, "Where is your picture?"

I looked up at my house behind Binh. Under my bed inside a cracked and peeling plastic card, a strange Western man wore grey robes. In one hand, he held a long tree branch, curved and pointing down. His other hand held a cross. I was frightened by his long beard and I seldom pulled him out from his hiding place.

At first, blood covered the plastic but over the

years it dried and flaked away. A thumbprint in blood once pressed upon the chest of the man but it too gradually faded.

Binh asked, "Do you ever think of the boy whose fingers held that image? Could it be his father? A farmer perhaps, with many buffalo?"

I thought for a moment and answered. "During my only trip to the South, I passed a Catholic church. A man sat behind a folding table selling pieces of paper. Thinking they were lottery tickets, I opened my pocket book to buy one."

"And one for me of course!"

"Of course, Honored Brother. As I handed him one hundred dong, I saw that the paper held not numbers but pictures, pictures of Western men and women in ancient costumes like our puppets wear in historical dramas. Among these many images lay the bearded man!

"The peddler seller saw my curiosity and said, 'Friend, I see you are on a journey from the country and as a Catholic your eyes are drawn to our holy Saint Christopher. He will protect you until you return home."

Binh asked, "Did the American soldier come from a famous family of priests, or do his people buy an image and pray for protection?"

I took his knight and added it to my pile. "Obviously the spirit in the picture did not do his job."

My brother studied his shrinking number of troops. "He would have been better off with a lottery ticket, perhaps."

"Yes, a strange people." I said. "They sent their

sons far away to die or go mad. Who will take care of their parents when they are old? Their family line is broken. There will be no new generation to honor their lives, no wisdom for new generations, and no memory of their passing."

Triggering an ambush, Binh placed my queen in jeopardy. "Why did they come?"

"These things I studied when I interrogated prisoners. They brought with them strange words, words the French did not bring. There is no translation and thus no understanding. Here, I wrote them in my memory book. "Democracy. Communism." Some kind of city government official perhaps. I do not know."

We stared at the chess pieces on the same board we used as boys, the same pieces when Binh had all his fingers and my wife and child still lived.

Binh sighed. "Well, at least we have peace now."

Around us, our longtime neighbors; poverty and illness, did not disagree.

Diary Excerpt
April 12, 1964
Son Vau Village

"Go get some oranges for Grandmother." Binh laughed and entered the front yard of his fiancé and her parents.

Grandmother's spirit voice echoed in my ear. "Buy the small plump ones. You know I love those!"

I turned onto the market road and away from the soccer field and my friends. Grandparents live with us at home but now only in black and white photos fading slowly away, just as they did in life.

My Apartment
Fredonia, New York, 1981
Vinh Lu, Interview Notes

Vinh stared out of my window at the falling snow. "One day, Mr. Mac, the images on photos will disappear completely but not until another generation becomes one with their stories, accomplishments, and most importantly, their names. No one dies in my homeland. Each day their names are on the lips and in the hearts of family and friends. Not to be remembered, not to continue contributing to future generations; to suffer such a fate would be as though one had never existed.

"Our people pray, not to a statue or image of a God nor do we practice ancestor worship as the French assumed. No invisible god such as the Catholic missionaries brought with them can contribute as our ancestors have, as the land does and as we will to our own descendents.

"These photographs conjure more than nostalgia. The wisdom they passed on to us emanates from these photos; their faces speak to us of the teaching and hold the center of our moral compass.

"We honor them daily with their favorite fruits, flowers, incense and a candle to symbolize the goodness they bring. The flow of generations moves through us, joined forever to the past and to the future of our own children.

"Any family member who is blessed to live

beyond a half century is revered as the repository of our collective life and is sought out for guidance in matters both public and private. We harvest these sweet fruits from the sages and cook a recipe for our own palate, satisfying our hunger for the divine in everyday life.

"My grandparents and their parents survived the Chinese Mandarins, the French, the Japanese and the French again. These barbarians came uninvited to our land. Each left, defeated by the ancient wisdom, stubbornness, and sacrifice of our ancestors.

"In our village few of us knew how to read, but this changed. The only gift of the French and their imperialist missionaries is their alphabet. We now use their system to read and write Vietnamese, replacing many complicated Chinese characters.

"During the occupation, the French collected men from our region disguised as a penalty for the failure to pay taxes. They forced them to labor for their plantations, forestry and railroad construction. Many conscripts never returned, or limped home as amputees, punishment for lack of cooperation during servitude.

"After a century, those hard days faded away along with the French. But as it has always been our fate, peace came to visit and stayed but a brief season.

Vinh stared into his tea cup. "Then you came, Mr. Mac."

Diary Excerpt
April 13, 1964
Son Vau Village

The oranges smelled delicious, full of the sweet goodness of our land and ripened by the waters of the Thu Bon. I was tempted. But as a child my knuckles were often red, rapped by my mother's weaving stick each time I reached for ripe offerings on the alter.

"Ah, here you are at last!" Grandma smiled at me from inside her picture on the altar.

Diary
April 20, 1966
Son Vau

Each evening around our village fire pit, we shared concerns. We saw no enemy, yet voices in river villages spoke of news from An Hoa to the east, of large machines tearing the skin off our land, destroying homes to make a place for airplanes. Where would the people live? How would they live? What of dignity? Stripped of ancestral fields and food, they must join other refugees, wandering.

A scraping sound in the dark announced the arrival of Trang. Leaning on his cane, he dragged his foot behind him and lowered his twisted body onto the log next to me. Both honored and shunned each day, Trang is a constant reminder of the torture and abuse of foreign occupation.

He laid his cane across his lap and as always, we listened. "This thing we must not do!"

Trang stared at each one of us sitting around the counsel fire. Such direct expression in public is permitted only by elders.

He stirred the fire with a stick and pointed at

our graveyard in the sacred plot. Smoke rose up from the end of the smoldering twig, drifted up through the trees, and disappeared.

"My great uncle cleared that land. I do not approve of digging up his bones so Northerners can tunnel and hide underground like assassins."

Stick in hand, Trang signed his death warrant. Informers were already among us. The harmony we had known in Son Vau was no more.

No one spoke. Trang spit his red beetle nut chew on the ground, rose, turned his back on us and hobbled into the darkness.

Diary Excerpt
May 1, 1966
Son Vau

Midday. Six of us stood in near darkness around his sleeping platform in the back of the hut. He lay motionless staring at patterns of thatch in the ceiling.

Binh tried his best. "You have your family, Trang and all of us will help."

"I cannot provide for my family. I am no longer a man. They should have taken my life. Not this!"

An arm rose up. Cloth used for filtering our drinking water covered his stump. Leather straps wound tightly around his right wrist.

"My work now? I am half man and half ghost who walks our village, a symbol of their Northern power, a half dead spirit to put fear into your hearts.

"You offer your help and my heart is full of gratitude." He looked away. "And full of shame. I am old and have seen much. This I say and then will say no more for my life is finished: They came for my hand and soon they will come for you."

Binh touched my elbow. We thanked Trang for his wisdom and walked home without speaking. Smoke from charcoal cooking fires drifted up and melted together, forming a grey cloud that gradually floated down over the river.

Mother stood waiting on the stone threshold of the front door.

"Did you bring the onions?"

Our hands held nothing. Trang filled our thoughts. I pointed at Binh, but too late. His finger was already up in position aiming at me.

"One of you get the bottle of nuoc mam from the creek and the other go find your story-telling father. I will use the sweet onions I was saving for your wedding, Vinh."

We turned in opposite directions and left on our assignments. Without looking, I knew Mother stood in the doorway arms folded over her heart's eye, watching her twin sons run off to play as she had for two decades.

My Apartment
Fredonia, 1981

Vinh pulled a tattered photograph from his shirt pocket. Outside, snow continued to fall.

"This is Mother." He slid her back into the pocket over his heart. "She died on the boat."

He stood and tried to smile, "One day I will look down upon my children from the wall in our American home and worry them with right thought and right behavior."

O'Doul's Pub
Fredonia, 1981

My thesis found approval and I graduated that same semester. To this day I reflect on the long reach of the God of War and wonder: will any of us who survived ever be free of His touch?

"Afghanistan:
The place where empires go to die. "

Anonymous

Russian Chorus

The letter arrived late one September morning just after he turned eighteen. There was nothing special about it, just another business sized envelope with his name.

Yet letters came rarely for Sasha. He noticed the envelope had no stamp. It didn't need one for the government didn't use stamps. Looking down at his name Sasha understood that his life had just changed, perhaps forever.

"Other guys in my class had received notices to report for active duty but Army wasn't taking everybody then and I thought somehow they might overlook me."

But Sasha wasn't overlooked. He reported for military training and along with others from his hometown was selected for an officer candidate program. After graduation joined a Special Forces group and with additional training shipped out. Seven months later his transport vehicle over a land mine in Afghanistan. With fragments of shrapnel still in his legs, he returned home to discover that not only the war but veterans too were unpopular.

Another American veteran, enlisted, wounded, and emotionally damaged? No. Sasha Tamarov was wounded twice in Helmond Provence, Jalalabad Afghanistan while serving with the Soviet Army in

106

1987.

Like our Vietnam, Iraq, and Afghanistan troops, his generation of soldiers, the "Afgansty", were sent to fight in a foreign country, against an invisible enemy and in a war that made no sense. In the USSR, combat survivors returned to an indifferent government and society to face the challenges of readjustment with little or no support.

Mac's Diary
Moscow, 1988

On November 6, 1988, a group of twenty-nine Americans gathered in Copenhagen and after a briefing flew on to Moscow. Organized by the Earth Stewards Network of Seattle, this coalition of veterans, psychologists, lawyers, specialists in artificial limbs, and organizers, formed a delegation to meet one on one with Soviet counterparts. Dr. Sandy Scull and I from Northern California joined the group.

Mac's Diary
Alma Ata People's Hospital

Outside the service entrance to the hospital, fog surrounded three men hovering about a small red sedan. Cement walls stared down and for a moment, we two Americans felt like criminals of the State. Someone was watching from somewhere, only allowing the drama to continue in the hope of entrapping more conspirators.

Sergey had been in the hospital now for ten or twelve minutes. Taking no chances, the car engine was running, and our getaway team paced the driveway trying to stay warm. Zhenya smoked while Sandy and I laughed nervously about the possible consequences of kidnapping a patient from the Alma Ata Peoples' Hospital. "Siberia! Sodium pentothal! Hard labor! Boiled potatoes!" Gruesome penalties indeed.

Sasha snuck out of the back door of the amputee wing with a paper bag of clothes. His friend had sworn to leave the hospital in time to meet with Vietnamsty who had come all the way to Alma Ata. This was his last chance.

Clanging metal doors burst open onto the loading dock. A crutch under each arm, blond hair crowning the victory smile of a boy playing hooky, Sasha looked down on his new comrades. Behind him, Sasha leaned against the door, nodding: a clean getaway.

The crutches stepped forward, Sasha's body followed. He no longer had legs. Heavy metal and leather limbs swung stiffly, leaving railroad tracks in the snow. He pulled to a stop in front of Sandy and me and reached out to hold us both in his iron grip.

We five vets squeezed into Zhenya's rusting sedan and roared off, challenging pedestrians all the way to Sasha's apartment. With no elevator, Sasha was the last one to join his homecoming on the second floor.

A well-dressed and sophisticated woman showed us into her sitting room. Oriental rugs, handsome furnishings, full bookshelves, and stereo components reflected the successful career of Sasha's wife, Lena, an assistant director of city planning.

Strength and feminine grace flowed from Lena as she attended to her husband's guests. The mutual love and respect and her pleasure in his homecoming felt like the presence of another person in the room.

Afgansty lyrics came to life out of the stereo. This now familiar music had become an overture from our ritual of sharing. After a toast with homemade vodka, Sasha opened his photo album. Lena, perhaps lamenting the continuing presence and celebration of war in her home, rose, and excused herself.

She studied these men who were still willing to feel good about their combat experiences, reminiscing over her coffee table, creating a new ritual she must play hostess to for years to come. Her husband sat propped up by pillows, again with brothers and new friends who understood him in a way she never could or ever wanted to. Lena turned and walked into her kitchen.

Sasha and I were alone on the couch, the others off to recruit a replacement for the now empty bottle of vodka.

He dealt his snapshots onto the table and identified friends and wartime circumstances. With identical memories and images, no translation was necessary. No language can describe such a moment.

My arm resting gently across the former commando's shoulders, I felt the pride and affection Sasha still held for his army career and comrades. Black-and-white memories covered the coffee table in front of us. Sasha became very still and gazed into a large color portrait on his lap. There, in full dress uniform, a decorated officer and leader of men in his prime...stood Sasha.

Captivated, he breathed in slowly, deeply. His full chest pushed him back into the couch, holding him erect. Turning to me, his soul full upon his face, he said with his heart, "Yes. This is the way I really am."

Quietly, involuntarily, Sasha's breath escaped, emptying him completely. With a small shrug, his smile returned and he looked down again at the photo he held in his hands. Reaching over the table, he dropped it face down on the pile of friends who hadn't made it home.

Another tray of food floated around the corner, followed by Lena. Her buoyant step hesitated as she felt the subtle change in her husband. Sasha lifted his head and squared his shoulders, once again becoming the attentive and cheerful host.

"We need room for tray!" Lena announced, and bent down over the coffee table. Gathering the photographs into their shoebox, she returned them to their closet, buried again, out of sight.

The Soviet trip accidentally deepened my understanding of PTSD. I traveled nine thousand miles to Moscow before meeting with American veterans, people with identical wartime experiences, feelings, and readjustment issues. Back in the States, some of the team members helped me navigate the maze of Veterans Administration red tape and receive assistance. Group and individual therapy followed; both good and bad, assholes and angels.

Money Talks
Marin County, CA

"What is a resume, Mister Mac?"

He was better dressed than his English, much more elegant than I. I handed him a folder.

"Here is an example. This person just got a job in San Francisco as an interpreter in the public schools. You can use that typewriter over there."

He stood gracefully and pressed his hands together in prayer. "Thank you, Mister Mac."

Our local satellite office of the Center for Southeast Asian Resettlement and Redevelopment held staff from five countries. My graduate degree, Vietnamese language, plus a gift for common sense deposited me behind a desk, finding jobs for refugees. Each day drama, comedy, and tragedy paraded through my office. What next?

The phone rang.

"That you, Mac?"

"Hi Cheng."

"You know the Vietnamese Trade Association is presenting products over in Frisco, right?" Always soft, his voice carried a subtle tone of intrigue. He knew how to work me.

"Yeah. You want to go?"

"Already did. Met a delegate who speaks Chinese and he wants to talk to you."

Cheng had the Chinese nose for profit and a refugee's flexibility with legal matters.

"OK. Bring him to my house for lunch. "

"We are in my car now. He must return by two.

No photos."

"See you there. You know where the key is."

This was gonna be good…

"Here is my resume, Mister Mac."

"You finished already, Tangen? "

He stood waiting as I read it over. "Says here you have been a military general, business man, yak herdsman, caravan master, and a slave. You look pretty young to have such a long work history."

He nodded. "These are jobs from my past lives. In this life I have been a monk and a teacher."

By then, my experiences with other cultures taught me to expect anything, so I kept a straight face, but I couldn't wait to tell the guys later down at the saloon.

"Tangen, the Berkeley Seminary is looking for a cultural informant and translator. I will set up an interview."

Trying to hide his pleasure, he bowed and floated out the way he came in.

Cheng had parked in my space so I pulled up on the lawn. Small, even for a Vietnamese, our guest stood when I entered. He wore the standard uniform of long sleeved white shirt and black slacks, both one size too big. A shoebox lay in the center of the kitchen table.

Cheng lubricated the introductions with hot tea, sliced orange sections, and his usual charm. "Mr. Tu requests his identity remain secret during negotiations."

For what?

"He knows you fought in the war, are a friend

of all soldiers, and know many people in Washington D.C."

I did? What was Cheng up to?

I smiled, nodded and sat down at Marin County's first negotiation with a man from the only country to defeat the United States in war.

Mr. Tu spoke to Cheng in a southern Chinese dialect. "He says he hopes to be your neighbor after he is granted political asylum. The weather reminds him of Hanoi."

The shoebox seemed to swell and grow larger. Cheng raised his eyebrows and asked a question. Tu reached across the table and lifted off the lid of the box. Fake Nikes? Stolen Rolexes?

Only a small packet wrapped in Chinese silk.

I got that old feelin'. The past lay there like a bad dream that just wouldn't go away. This time the nightmare was nicely packaged in red silk: the Chinese symbol for lucky money.

Tu slowly rolled out the fabric with delicate fingers which no doubt set booby traps not too long ago. He spread out four items and sat back in his chair.

Apparently, he had memorized one English sentence. "Two million dollar, Mister Mac. Some you, some Cheng Lim."

Looking back at me from my kitchen table, four souvenirs from Vietnam: dog tags, a hand written letter, an old photo, and a severed finger. In those days we all knew of the standing reward for evidence proving the existence of a live POW.

Cheng shattered my trance. "Mr. Tu will be here with the trade mission until Saturday. We may keep these things as proof of a POW but you must not reveal his identity even after sanctuary is granted. Communist cadre came into Northern California concealed in the second wave of immigration."

Jesus! I probably got some of them jobs. "OK, Tu. I know someone." But who?

He relaxed for the first time and sipped some tea, his two hands around an Asian cup with no finger loop. Staring out the front window, he scanned the houses on my street, no doubt seeing himself with a new family living on an American street of gold.

Cheng looked at his watch and nodded in the direction of the Golden Gate Bridge. The bounty hunter and I stood up and walked to the door. "Chao Anh, Ong Mac."

"Chao Anh, Ong Tu."

From the porch, I watched the pickup truck pull away. Ripples of our war spread across time and touched us as it always would.

My house held no memorabilia on the walls, no photos of Marine buddies in an album, no uniform hanging in the back of the closet and no medals stashed in the back of a dresser drawer. What did I have? Total immersion in the refugee community as a job counselor for South Vietnamese Army vets, housing agent for elderly refugees and a Vietnamese girlfriend.

Every day I witnessed the Southeast Asian international resettlement games: Catholic vs. Buddhist, North vs. South, educated vs. villager, nationalist vs. royalist, and all the variations. Fate had placed me in the role of codependent, confidant, and

114

sometimes co-conspirator as new arrivals sought out a sympathetic power broker and advocate, matching their own cultural model .

I looked over at the severed finger on the table. Now what? Maybe Ben Johnson was over at the bar lecturing to tourists until 86ed at the end of the afternoon. I picked up the phone.

Judy answered, "He's gone home, thank God!"

Twenty minutes later I left Inverness behind and headed north for Johnson's Oyster Ranch on nearby Tomales Bay. Old trailers, doublewides, funky sheds, and a funky retail storefront stood like a backdrop from a hillbilly movie.

Surrounded by dairy and cattle ranches of the original Portuguese, Italian, and Irish homesteads, strings of cultivated oysters hovered in cold waters. Up on the porch, Ben sat in his throne: an old wicker chair with wings on each side. Lieutenant Numbnuts, his bodyguard lay next to him on his porch. He didn't have to bark. Ben took care of that job.

Through a flattened and often-broken nose he snorted, "What'd you want?"

During our first encounter in the Western Saloon he "made" me as a combat vet. I too felt that special affinity, and our intimacy grew over both beers and time. Was I the only one who knew? All his stories were true.

Too many years in covert and black operations had wounded him deeply, and there would be no return for Ben from the shadows. A mask of cynicism hid a heart of gold as he played town drunk. Beer and isolation kept the shadow daemons on the other side of the concertina wire. Both of us were the same age. He looked twenty years older.

Ben believed in an America that no longer existed. He championed the underdog, smuggled and employed illegal aliens from three countries, contributed to homeless shelters, and bought drinks for any and all. His bayside business was worth a million and a half.

I looked around the oyster camp. A couple of heads popped out of the window in the shucking shack where I taught English on Thursday nights. Always hyper-vigilant, employees knew much more English than they showed.

"Ben, you still have a contact in the Pentagon?"

He read my concern and placed his beer down on top of the cooler.

"Why?"

"Can we go inside?"

"Follow me." Never as drunk as he pretended, we navigated a minefield of empties and entered the trailer with Lt. Numbnuts trailing behind.

A card table stood in the kitchen area and soon held two Budweiser. "Sit down. OK. Whatcha got?"

I pushed aside a bag of Cheetos and dropped the packet on the table. Ben pulled out bifocals, sat up straight and opened the silk. The finger spilled out, rolled around a bit and lay there, pointing at him.

He reached into pile on the counter and pulled out a magnifying glass. "Finger print is long gone. What else is in here?"

His own past appeared and laid there like three tombstones: dog tags, a letter, and a photo. A Filipino employee in my class had whispered, "Mr. Ben, he prisoner in communist camp, Mindanao. Very bad!"

He read the letter while the finger still pointed his way. Curmudgeon, cynic, and tough old bird, Ben Johnson laid his head down on the table and cried. Lt. Numbnuts whined, rose up and put his head in Ben's lap, standing guard until this most recent assault from the past faded.

A minute passed. Unashamed, Ben wiped his nose with the bag of Cheetos. "This way."

His bedroom held a strange mix of Asian art, carved knick-knacks, old photos, bookshelves full of philosophy, classical literature, a half finished oil canvas on an easel tripod, and a huge pile of gold Krugerrrands on top of the dresser. Stacked against the wall, and next to a bed that hadn't been made since the Battle of Hue City, stood three rifles, all clean and shiny, all converted to full automatic.

In the far corner, Ben picked up an old circular dial phone and pulled the cylinder all the way round. "Operator, I want to place a collect call to the Pentagon, 7036971776, General Xxxx. Tell him it's Ben Johnson."

He looked back at me and wiggled a finger. Was this really happening? I moved to his side. Behind me, Lt. Numbnuts growled.

"Yes General, it's Ben. Fine, thank you Sir. General I have a man here with some Intel on a possible POW. I can vouch for him."

He turned and pushed the receiver at me.

"Hello General."

"What have you got, son?" He sounded like a

general.

I described the contents of the packet and how they came to be in my possession.

The man in the pentagon was not impressed. "Yes. These types of submissions are more frequent now that travel to Vietnam has been loosened up. Photograph everything and send it to me. Ben has the address. And tell that sonofabitch commie gook to get a photo of our POW holding next week's copy of the International Times available in Vietnam. Then we're on to something. Now give me Ben."

"Yes Sir."

I needed a beer so I returned to the kitchen, sat back down at the card table, and grabbed a cold one from the cooler. Lt. Numbnuts stared at me from the bedroom, keeping score.

Ben dropped a business card on the table. "Here's the address for the photos. Give it back after you send the stuff." Four stars stood in formation under a D.C. address. "And don't say a damn word."

"OK Ben." I tossed down the rest of the Budweiser. "I gotta get this stuff back to the trade rep."

He pulled a dusty photo off the wall and stared at small squad of guerilla fighters. "We taught those gook assholes good."

He opened another beer and toasted the photo. "Now they're sellin' our memories."

"Cursed by my tribe, if I forgive him"
The Merchant of Venice
Shakespeare

Echoes
Nong Son, Vietnam

After 32 years, 6500 miles, 3 airplanes, and 4 hours in a rusty Russian sedan, familiar rice paddies and tree lines appear alongside a wide brown river. Mopeds and a few more people roam the frontage road, yet this fertile valley is almost unchanged in the photo album of my mind.

Our car slows, stops. I'm here. Standing on the sandy shore of the Thu Bon, I stare across the wide river at the village of Nong Son and into yesterday. Why have I returned after all these years?

Rich Hoffman and I set out on May 5 of this year to recapture Vietnam. Our tour of duty will be three weeks. This time we are tourists heavily armed with dollars. Four years of working with Vietnamese refugees in California, and my role as a Marine interpreter left me with positive cross-cultural experiences and memories. How bad could it be?

Nine long months in the infantry and the Marine Corps sent me to live alone in the village of Nong Son. My role as an English teacher and liaison with the South Vietnamese militia would require winning the support of villagers. It was hoped I might be supplied with intelligence to fight the Viet Cong in Quang Nam Province.

Now, only Asian profiteers in search of hard

wood forests venture this deep into the interior. As we travel along the back roads, wonder and humor on the faces 0f farmers working in the paddies stare back at us. Most rural Vietnamese look at tourists with frank curiosity and respond smile for smile.

The dignity found in these traditional communities replaces the city hustlers, beggars and vendors. Blond, physically fit, and dressed in Tae Kwan Do attire, Rich draws a small crowd each time we exit the car.

In the mountains now we are swept away by lush and sensual memories pulling us into the past; the harsh perfume of noontime cooking fires, bright conical hats floating over green rice fields, sing-song voices bargaining raw meat, sweat and humidity- all mix together melting away the years. My feet want to walk down the middle of a rice paddy. Are the adrenaline rush and paranoia still there just under the surface?

Nong Son village stands at the bottom of a 2000-foot hill. White, blue, and green colonial French buildings in orderly rows still survive, saluting the patience of the Vietnamese in three wars of liberation. Our Marine security company once ran patrols from here and commanded the valley with mortars placed on top of the hill. Military historians would later characterize the Marine defense of Vietnam's only working coal mine as 'symbolic' with acceptable losses.

The same ferryman from years ago approaches. Thin and brown moving in slow rhythm, it's hard to distinguish arms and legs from his pole and long-handled rudder. He smiles as he did so long ago, but now his ancient skull strains against leathery skin impatient for its turn. He poles the boat closer to shore. Rich, our interpreter Mr. Chin and I climb in. Carved from a tree trunk, the long slender canoe glides across the murky water and into the past. For many Marines this would become The River Styx.

Drifting across the silky brown Thu Bon I gaze downriver. Once, we won the hearts and filled the pocketbooks of fishermen by dropping grenades to stun fish and bringing them to the surface. Later, the same fishing boats dropped us at launch points for patrols or ambushes into the valley.

Gently, the canoe touches the opposite shore. We step out and onto the soil of Nong Son. I'm here. I'm back, and for a moment, young again. It's 1967. I'm stepping off the metal ferryboat that conveys my platoon into Nong Son on July 1. Then I carried 70 pounds on top of a flak jacket. Today I am sweating with a light rucksack and tee shirt. I look down expecting to see jungle boots and watch tennis shoes sink into the red mud.

Can I find my old plaster house? Is the classroom still intact? Will the students now middle aged, recognize me? So many happy memories in the midst of war and chaos; Vietnamese writing pen pal letters to my old high school, medical treatment for villagers, Marine vs. villagers in volley ball and soccer, intimate and clandestine discussions of war, politics and ethics in our secluded classroom and ultimately, my acceptance into this remote village near the Cambodian border.

Our small group approaches the first buildings. Army officers in the same gray-green wartime uniforms and pith helmets step out onto the veranda and gesture to us to climb up the stone stairs. A red metal star flashes from a belt buckle.

Our charming and effervescent Mr. Chin suddenly becomes passive, obedient. Directed to enter a small office, we sit around a small circular table with the officers standing above, staring down. We wait. A cross cultural standoff. Overhead, a tired fan slices through afternoon heat. Who are we? The hotel has our passports. Phone calls are made. Thirty minutes pass. Hyper vigilant, Rich scans the mood, exits, and river below. Identities are verified.

Why are we here? To visit my wartime station. No American has ever returned here. Nong Son is not on the official tourist list. More phone calls. This time to Hanoi.

Mr. Chin does his best to lubricate the tension in the room, but he is in deep water and obviously afraid. Slowly curiosity wins out over suspicion and boredom. When will these men stationed in such an isolated region get a chance like this again? Tea and cigarettes are presented. I place a box of American Marlboros on the table. Mr. Chin finally relaxes and begins to translate capitalism into communism.

I sip perhaps the strongest tea ever poured. As a foreign invader and former occupier of Nong Son, the army personnel are interested in my experiences and perspective. Hoping to retrieve my story without providing any information of their own, they begin to gently probe. More employees and troops collect in the windows and doorway. We are yesterday come back, tall pale ghosts haunting those old enough to remember.

The Vietnamese officials are concerned that I may understand their conversation. Vietnamese is a tonal language and my ear IS of out of tune. Most of it passes by and blends with the squeaking of the fan overhead. Captain Kiet asks what intelligence I was able to collect while an "operative school teacher." Humor seems the best choice. "I was both young and stupid and found out only one thing! I liked teaching and it has been my career." Laughter. They appreciate evasion.

Captain Kiet feels more comfortable. He smiles, keeping his hand on my forearm. I remember adult male students walking home and holding hands with me along the street outside this same window. Scary the first time. He suggests that we may be able to stroll along the frontage road and walk ten meters into the village.

Am I man enough to hold hands?

Mr. Chin exhales. He may earn his bonus yet. We rise, march down the steps and head into the ville. Over there is the volleyball court where Marines beat the villagers. Adjacent is the soccer field where the Vietnamese ran circles around the taller, heavier Americans. Behind the playing field is the classroom where students thrilled to my nonexistent teaching skills.

The Nong Son coalmine is now a government run and Army administered operation. The entire former population was relocated after the War of

Liberation. A few of the stucco buildings received new paint, but all the landmarks, buildings and huts stand there exactly as they did in 1967. Few returning American veterans will find such a moment. Most former US sites suffered fates similar to our old battalion base at An Hoa. A name change in 1975 was not enough. An Hoa is now underwater as the result of new dam construction.

Nong Son. Where are the former children and adults? Both taught me how to reclaim my humanity in the middle of the killing fields. They are scattered now, just like the Marines once stationed on Nong Son Hill, each completing their own destiny. For many, their lives ended on patrol, others as "collateral damage" or at midnight July 4, 1967, as VC overran the hilltop.

Captain Kiet takes my hand and leads me to a side street and walks us uphill half a block. We peek around the corner and I see my old plaster apartment attached to the end of a row of identical units. My room, where we had a Halloween party and bobbed for mangoes, where adults cried when I translated letters from their American pen pals. My room, where I wrote letters to the parents of dead friends from Foxtrot Company. Is my journal still buried under the floor? I'd like to read the thoughts and feelings of the young man I used to be.

As we walk back the way we came I hand Captain Kiet a small package of a dozen "exotic" American vegetable and fruit seeds. "My friend. These are from my family to your family. When I come back next year, I want some rutabaga pudding."

124

Looking at the picture of a rutabaga on the seed packet, he shakes his head and then laughs. We stop and stare up at the top of Nong Son Hill where Foxtrot was overrun. Who won? Brutality.

"Mr. Mac, I apologize, your old friends not here." Captain Kiet is sad for the first time, thinking perhaps also of lost comrades. The two of us stand with one foot in the past and another in the moment. He brings us back to the present.

"Perhaps we make new friends today."

Coming down the road is a dignified and well-dressed man of fifty. He is hard to read but the news he carries cannot be good. Captain Kiet assumes his official persona. "Mr. Mac, I introduce you Mr. Kinh. He fight against your group top of hill. He last one here living."

Mr. Kinh's eyes bore into me. I want to share a beer, discuss battle tactics, small-unit action and personal survival. Healing, reconciliation, a psychic cease-fire. You know, like on "60 Minutes".

This former freedom fighter feels something far different. Polite and stiffly formal, he offers his hand but there is no connection. There are only two men reaching across the years, each with old wounds, some yet to heal.

Offended I have returned a second time Mr. Kinh turns and walks back into his village to his people and his own past.

Minutes later the canoe leaves the shore and I look over my shoulder. Nong Son is still there, different now but forever the same. In midstream, I pull papers from my rucksack and read the lists one

125

last time. In my hands are the names of all the Foxtrot Marines killed in action; one hundred and forty-two. Gently, lovingly, I tear the papers into many pieces and release them to the waters of the Thu Bon.

Back now in Hanalei, my skin is brown from the sun over Quang Nam Province, and the red mud of Vietnam is still on my shoes. I live quietly at the end of town beside a river. It's muddy most of the time. Some nights when the wind blows down from the mountain and rain beats a rhythm on the broad leaves outside my window, I hear again that dark music from another time, another place.

Part V
The Pen

Voices in the Shadows
Phuket, Thailand

Dear Mac,

A couple nights ago there was some gunshots coming from the big nursery next door someone walking around and capping random shots into the night. I was up and out, down the road (walkin' trail) to see where the source was. No sleep, kept checkin' perimeter.

Mai found me sittin' on the floor in the kitchen doorway 6 a.m. coffee in hand. She hugs me and asks me what am I doing up so early?

I told her about the shooting. Said I feel like I'm back in Nam. Guess my face went strange at that point as she asked me what's wrong. Hugs me tighter. Tears comes.

I'm coping, telling myself it's a good thing. Maybe shed some pounds outta that old rucksack in my head.

Bro D

Dear D,

The war within continues......we can only hope for a cease-fire. Be well, my friend. You are seen and loved. Keep a light on in the window (you do have windows, right?) A poem for you...

Shadows

Not too far
from the old
free fire zone,
his suburban bunker
built by native labor
and staffed with
Asian love,
stands alone
against the night.

Now
the last man standing
patrols his past
in yesterday's moonlight
seeking Psyche's sniper
but can't...
make contact.

And under memory's assault
his elaborate perimeter
dissolves around him
while he performs
his own autopsy
on the kitchen table
washing his wounds-
in his own tears

Mac

Conversation with the Past
San Diego, California

Mac,

I received quite a few pictures from xxxxx of this year's Fox 2/5 reunion in Washington, DC and I thought I would pass them on to you to view on line when you have time.

For me one revelation was a the 2nd Platoon's Machine Gun Team. Cpl. xxxxx team was in attendance. Cpl. xxxxx went home about two weeks before Union II and he asked me "What the hell happened?.

I told him the Skipper did the right thing and wanted to prep the area with air then artillery. You know the whole story. I told him Colonel Hilgartner refused the Skipper's request and gave him a direct order to move the company out into the open or the "meat grinder" if you will.

I told him the story in front of Major General xxxxx, he was the CO of Fox in xxxx. Two of Cpl. xxxxx's men said they listened to the transmission between the Skipper and me and both said there wasn't anything I could have done to change the outcome.

With all this said I still never feel quite right because I think I could have changed the outcome if I had not obeyed the Skipper's orders.

Well my friend we have talked about this same subject for years and the outcome will never change. I'm sorry you missed being at the reunion. As I see the shape of some of our brethren I fear they will not

be at the next reunion. If there is something I can do for you please let me know.
Semper Fidelis
Sarge

Dear Sarge,

Your wife looks great and your smile fills the room as usual.

Thanks so much for thinking of me and the photos, just what I was hoping for, a bit of sit rep from the reunion. I recognize some of the guys and appreciate the tour of DC. Some of the scenes bring a wave of emotion and I feel tears forming in the eyes of a young man who once had a band of brothers like no other.

As for you my friend, there is a well known story to share with you and I have changed it a little to fit our purposes here.

… A man who has lived a life of integrity and service, sits alone in his back yard as the sun goes down and shadows begin to dance across a tree line in the distance. After reviewing the many accomplishments of his life, he smiles and attempts to stand but that familiar ache pulls him back down...... the demon of regret.

In the shadows before him, a spirit appears and offers him a reward for a life well lived. "Sergeant, you can return to that moment which haunts you even now after all these years. You will be as you were then with one difference: you will have the consciousness of this time and know the consequences of choices made then. Do you want to go back?"

130

A little over weight and burdened still with many responsibilities, he responds as he always has, "Let's do it!"

Instantly he is transformed into the young man he once was and around him, stand even younger Marines under his command, locking and loading in a tree line. In front of them a dry, rocky, rice paddy stretches out; a graveyard waiting. Over the radio and in a voice he can barely recognize, his beloved Captain hesitates, then says, "No prep Tony. Move out. The CP will provide cover and reserve."

His heart breaks. For the first time as a Marine, the Sergeant refuses an order. "Captain, we all know this is wrong. I just can't do it, not till Arty and Air saturate the area across and above the paddy."

Silence. Then...

"Yes. You are right. I'll pass it up to Battalion."

A week later in the Stars and Stripes, a headline reads, "Operation Union II, major disaster. Hesitation results in USMC, 1st Battalion, 5th Regiment surrounded and wiped out."

It's dark and the Sergeant is again sitting in his backyard. But something is missing a pain so old it had become another part of him, and a companion he'd felt he must carry to his grave.

Shining and barely visible, the spirit stands before him in the darkness and asks, "You understand now. We can never know the consequences of changing the events of that moment or any other in the past. But you can still change your own past. You can let it go..."

The spirit dissolves into the night and with him, the Sergeant's ancient pain.

Brother, we can never really know what might have happened on that day if we had made other choices. Many of us had that gut feeling it was all wrong, and each of us is still processing in our own way... I cried more than once and at another time called Col. Xxxxx at his retirement home in Virginia and raged.

You are still alive, fighting the good fight, have created a model family and lived a life like few others. It is enough, more than enough. Captain Graham looks down and he is so very proud of you. As am I.

Your Brother,
Mac

Epiphany
Face Down

Operation Union II, from May 15 to June 5th, 1967, is documented as one of the bloodiest battles in the long years of war. In the late afternoon of June 2nd, a U-shaped ambush decimated Foxtrot. I lay face down in a dry rice paddy, alone and unarmed, while a machine gun sprayed rounds back and forth. "The Moment" had arrived. I waited for revelation. Nothing.

Now what? Try a prayer? OK. "Dear, Whoever or Whatever. I don't want anything but if there is something going on that I don't know about, would you give me a little sign? Maybe a lightning bolt or something'?"

Nothing. Bullets kept coming.

Then I understood. This moment is all there is, full of Life It Self, every human possibility and choice. As I received this obviously tardy revelation, the sniper stopped firing. Transformed, I relaxed and for the first time in memory, ready to live without doubt or the feeling that something was missing.

Suddenly, I floated above the rice paddy and saw my body lying below in the midst of carnage and chaos. My twenty three years of confusion, mistakes, missed opportunities and immature distractions stretched out in a long trail as though I had navigated a carefully constructed career path. All that time, energy and wasted potential to wind up as a colossal fool hugging a dirt clod nine thousand miles from home.

I laughed and reunited with my body. I had known a few seconds of peace before death. The explosions, roar of aircraft and gunfire faded away. Twilight approached. I watched a red tracer round whizz back along the path in the direction the ancient past of the morning.

My tormentor stopped firing. I lay quietly in the dirt, waiting for night.

Epitaph
Above the Pacific

On the commercial flight back home and separated from my Foxtrot Company brothers I was surrounded by strangers, yet strangers feeling many of the same emotions, holding on to the similar images...

All those dead teenagers we left behind; so full of energy, each ready for a new and more deeply appreciated life upon returning home.

We survivors knew: the only real meaning in our war was loyalty to and support of one another. Over the following years this would become our only cherished legacy from that distant place and time.

Halfway across the Pacific a vision came to me. Inspired, somehow born again, I reenlisted for a new tour of duty. My mission? To forever hold within me the faces and images of Foxtrot Marines killed in action. If they were forgotten, then truly, their young lives and sacrifice meant nothing.

My promise to the Dead: "To carry your spirit forward and contribute to the well being of others. I will not let the torch of your memory burn low and go out. To do so will result my own spiritual death."

Back in the jungle, a squad of Viet Cong squatted in a circle, grinned and reached for another handful of rice. Their last and most insidious booby trap had been set and smuggled into a duffle bag, the one inside my head.

Enemy Mine
Ragheads, Hadjis, Gooks
Dinks, Krauts and Japs:
Grunts!

Perhaps one day our most recent veterans will find a way to connect peacefully with their own personal Arab waiting to ambush them in their dreams, flash backs and intrusive thoughts. Until then, continuing to believe an entire race, religion and culture was and is the enemy, damages only the well being of the believer and his/her chance of ending the war within and returning all the way home.

After the Soviet pullout from Afghanistan, a small group of Afgansty received permission from both countries to return as civilians. Two friends of Sasha Tamarov led a group of Afgansty combat veterans to rebuild an apartment complex destroyed by Soviet gunfire some years before. Half of the volunteers had been stationed in the same town during their tour of duty.

In February of 1988, the California based Vietnam Restoration Project sent their first team of twelve Vietnam veterans back to "help build that which they had helped to destroy." A medical clinic was built in the seacoast town of Vung Tau. This was the first in the ongoing program to build public service structures in Vietnam. The value of 'reconstruction' projects is a therapeutic healing process for Soviets, Americans and former soldiers of the countries affected by war.

Luftwaffe and RAF pilots from WWII have

been meeting for decades. At reunions they discuss personal encounters in the skies over Europe and survival. Old demons are buried and comrades not present, remembered. Japanese and American infantry troops who fought against each other in the Pacific theater now land on island beaches to erect monuments memorializing their comrades.

For years I worked as a job developer and ESL instructor with the Center for South East Asian Resettlement and Redevelopment plus another refugee agency. Civil wars such as Vietnam and our own Civil War are the most damaging to the soul and psyche as we fight to slay our own physical, mirror image.

Unknown to our State Department, North Vietnamese Army veterans smuggled themselves and their families into relocation camps and immigrated to California. Their struggle to build a new life became the priority and their efforts to help their own community included those willing to forgive. The war was over and survivors bonded by the same trauma learned to work together.

Expendable
From Cannon Fodder
To Guinea Pig

It is time to pause for just a moment and remember that over two million Americans have served in our two most recent wars. Many have returned with physical or psychological wounds, some with both. Thousands are dead. But there is good news.

The 'D' has been dropped from Post Traumatic Stress Disorder! Active duty personnel and veterans are no longer branded as suffering from a Disorder. We are simply victims of PTS: Post Traumatic Stress. Even more progress in labeling can be found among creative clinicians who now offer treatment in PTG: Post Traumatic Growth. I feel better already.

The traditionally conservative *American Legion Magazine*, (October 11, 2011), printed an article on PTS and alternative roads to recovery. Once again, media put a positive spin on PTSD by highlighting the most recent therapeutic trend in this expanding industry: the hyperbaric oxygen chamber. While initial benefits of this pilot program are encouraging, long term value is unknown, costs prohibitive and as for availability? When is the last time you saw or even heard of a compression chamber?

In a widely publicized survey in December of 2011, one in three members on active duty in the Middle East finds their war not worth fighting. Patriotism? Each day here and abroad, young men and women are victims of seventeen suicides within our military family and these are the *reported* figures.

Despite a PR program launched after the expose of conditions at Walter Reed Hospital claiming improvements in treatment for veterans and active duty personnel, any on-line chat room with current military personnel and veterans (try Hulu) testifies to the ongoing adversarial relationship between both groups and the Veterans Administration.

Yet there are opportunities offered by the system. During a recent visit to the VA Medical Hospital at Fort Miley in San Francisco, I walked by a bulletin board. Half a dozen posters and flyers called out to any veteran, diagnosed (and undiagnosed) with PTSD and addicted to drugs. We can now find gainful employment. Job descriptions? Submit to electrical stimulation and doses of experimental pharmaceuticals administered no doubt by post Big Pharma interns who can't find Afghanistan on a map.

Pay ranges from $50-$240 per study. Contact these employment opportunities at 415 221- 4810, extensions; 4145, 3103 and 2752. Give 'em a call.

Epilogue
Who's the Teacher?

"Today we write our own obituaries. You guys almost died bunch of times, so no big deal. Here, take a look at some samples from the local paper."

Silence. Stares. Jeez, was the whole group on meds? I tried to lighten it up...

"Think about it. We survived not only war but coming back home and trying to fit in. Do you want someone else telling everybody who you are and what to remember about you?"

Some of the guys perked up a bit and looked at the handout. One or two grabbed a pencil. Time for my brilliant idea...

"Let's start with tombstones. Jot down what words you want standing over you for eternity. Look at page two and you'll see some photo copies of a dozen so tombstones and their inscriptions."

Boy, I had 'em now... "At the bottom of the page is the outline of a tombstone with six blank lines inside. Pretend it's yours and you are filling in a purchase order."

Sonny scribbled for a second, tossed his pencil on the table, stood and limped out the door. His buddy from group therapy leaned over and read the inscription. "Says, "I died in Vietnam." He peered over the top of his glasses. "Don't worry Mac, he always comes back. He's got nowhere else to go."

Across our table, Lenny clicked the trigger on his Marine Corps League ball point pen. "Think I'll write something about being the only Asian in boot camp and them usin' me as an example of how enemy gooks looked." He pointed his pen at me. "I got it!"

Lenny stabbed his worksheet and started writing. After a couple of seconds he sat up and grinned around the circle. "How's this sound? 'You happy now? P.S., Fuck you!'"

Everybody cracked up and reached for their handouts.

I got out of the way. "OK, let's all do our own. Me too. Don't worry about making sense, spelling or grammar. Just keep the pens moving and don't stop until you finish."

So we began our first day of, *Expressive Writing for Combat Veterans.* In the next two hours forgotten feelings and memories flowed out from new places within each writer. We read aloud to each other and left class a bit lighter and a little less alone.

At the end of two hours I stuffed worksheets into my old briefcase and checked in with the director. He leaned back in his chair and folded his hands together over his stomach. "You seem, different."

"It's the strangest thing, Steve. Feels like I just came home from a very long trip. We are all very different in that room but we know what the other guy is going to say before it's spoken."

He nodded. "They have just initiated you into an exclusive club. While you present well and are cast in the role of 'teacher', they smell another combat vet just as wounded and potentially crazy as they are." He laughed. "Should I schedule class for next week?"

I looked at the photo of his recon team in Vietnam hanging on the wall behind him. "Sure."

Honolulu sun burned hot as I left the Vet Center and headed down the sidewalk to the parking lot. Two hours of war stories, poems, confessions and failures on the road back home still echoed in my head, pulling me into Vietnam and my own shit. Did I really want to do this?

From behind, a yellow hand grabbed my shoulder. I turned. Wild slanted eyes with dilated pupils, magnified by thick lenses and an anti-depressant, stared into me. Lenny Ho, Marine combat veteran and Gate Keeper between Light and Dark, knew that many of us needed to be welcomed back home, every day.

He squeezed, "Don't worry, Mac, we'll take care of you."

Elegy
The Brotherhood of Men

Rings I have, watches, tokens, a dog tag
To take back to the land of the living
From the dead to deliver to fathers and sisters,
Cherished possessions of my luckless companions
Lost in four years of abuse.
Oh to forget, forget the fever and famine,
The fierceness of visions, the faith beyond reason,
To forget man's lot in folly of man.
And swear never to kill a living being.
To live for love, the lost country of man's longing.

And yet I know a knowledge unspeakable
That we were at our peak when in the depths.
Lived close to life when culled by death,
Had visions of brotherhood, when we were broken,
Learned compassion beyond the curse of passion,
And never in after years those left to live
Would treat with truth as in those savage times,
And sometimes wish that they had died
As did those many… crying in their arms.

Richard Eberhart
Infantry, WWII

143

Exorcism
The Mighty Pen

So what about this expressive writing thing? Is it just another scam to sell a book? And yes, there are more PTSD self help manuals than you can shake a twenty dollar bill at. You've heard my voices, read my flash backs and listened to my intrusive thoughts. But it's time to talk about the voice in *your* head and only you can do that. You know, the one who keeps calling you to places where you don't want to go. How do you stop or slow down that conversation and perhaps one day agree on a cease fire?

Try this: sit quietly and invite those thoughts, images and feelings in. Make it OK to listen, feel, remember the dark side for the next few minutes. Let the voice rant and rave as it brings its shit storm.

Pick up a pen or place your fingers on a keyboard and transcribe the monologue you just heard. If it's an image, find an old photograph of the person or place or draw a picture as best you can. Take your time. Capture it! Hold the words or image, prisoner on a piece of paper in your hands. Fold it neatly and place it in an envelope. Seal it. Address it to that place, person or experience haunting you. Find a special area in your back yard, a barbeque pit in a park or your fire place. Now burn it!

Watch the smoke rise and evaporate. Say some words during the cremation: a farewell speech, because this muthafucker is dying and will soon be dead. Some shadows are hard to kill. If you get ambushed again, burn 'em till they're gone!

Part VI
Poems

I Cannot Wait in Vain

My darling
I can't take this anymore.
I only know my little life.
A diamond reveals its full worth
When shining in the darkness,
Inflaming sweet happiness.

I only want to hear poetry as the sun sets;
I promise I will be loving, faithful.
Our laughter will ring out in every direction.
I only want to watch the autumn sun set,
Your heart beating next to mine.

Our renewed life will arrive
on the morning wind,
Once the clouds pass by.

From the diary of a
dead NVA Soldier
Khontum Diary
Paul Reed

Save Our World

Beyond the horizon,
I can see the dusk
About to cover my pious world.
From all the lights my world
Passed by, her people drag
Not my mother to darkness.

To be heard, blowing missiles and bombs
Is just a nerve-breaking affair.
Stop my brothers wherever
You live. Our mother is same,
The same breast we suckle,
On the same lap we sleep

by Raghab

Chips in the Mint

"More ice cream Honey?"
Dark, shrapnel eyes
chocolate chips
in the mint,
stare back
through yesterday's
green mist.

Inside...
the kitchen wallpaper
of shiny ribbons
hiding jungle bamboo,

....inside Honey,
splattered bodies
of old friends
....and enemies,
wait.

Back in this land,
feasting on shallow
suburban calories,
he starves-
a hungry,
empty life
surrounded in this time,
by a banquet
of fools.

Around him,
His defensive perimeter
of a neighborhood bunker,
fades away each Sunday
behind a smoke screen
of Bar-b-que'd,
burning flesh.

Honey slices only
civilized meat now
carving
yesterday's
body count
into his own,
friendly fire,
ribs.

He's camouflaged
inside,
a flak jacket of fat.
Unable now to bend,
baste his kill
he sighs,
surrenders-
ready to join
memories,
carved
up there-
on The Wall.
Mac

John McCain Pretends
Maverick!
Dad's fault…
maybe Grandpa's.
But I showed 'em!
North Vietnamese beating me?
No problem.
I just relaxed,
felt the legacy
of Admiral McCain.

Torture?
Familiar family territory.
Bombing Hanoi?
Women and children?
I imagined
my family estate,
below.

Shot down, floating
in that famous rice paddy?
Ah, born again,
baptized,
free of expectations.

Five years captive?
A gift of penance
to expiate
the sins
of this favorite Son
miscast
as heir apparent.

Here in my portable cell
still a prisoner,
I fight on,
always counter punching,
fighting ghosts,
warrior without a war.

The gooks?
My friends...
they could have broken me
with just a little...kindness.

Mac

Sons of Abraham
This Gaza trip
The knife of our Father
Carves out
This silent space

Between us.

This separation from God:
Our original sin,
Cast us out
From Eden
And we turn our backs
On Paradise.

Someone else
Now lives our lives..
Locked inside,
Mad Men pace,
Feet tick-tocking
Around perimeters,
Protecting....
Nothing.

On the long road back
To segregated Bethlehem,
Brother slays brother
And we watch
Our self -inflicted wound
Bleed out into a gutter
Along this common artery
Reunited, at last

Mac

John Kerry Has a Cup of Coffee
"Refill, Darlin'
or
are you OK?"

Armed
with standard issue smile,
waitress hovers
over his sector-
of the counter.

Her civilian tongue
tastes the testimonial
on the chalkboard,
"Today's Special!
Piece of Mind"

Swift aluminum shape
glides to his cup
delivering a hot payload.
Steam rises from the brew,
blending Sunday morning sounds.

Ancient essence
in an instant
of C-ration coffee,
consumes him...
again.

His back to the wall now,
cup in both hands,
he stares across the room,

over the black pool
and scouts through
yesterday's mist
as village families
single file to
empty vacant places.

Every thing
as it should be-
every thing
as it was-
every thing
in place,
everything...
'Out of Order'.

Double doors explode
and open
A bus boy charges,
pointing his grey tub
and rescues dirty casualties
from the morning's operation.

Busboy white
fades to army green,
Vietnamese Boy.

From the dark crystal
in his cup,
steam swims up
burning his eyes.
"Approaching the LZ,

Lieutenant.
Your team ready?"

Behind the counter
toast burns
and closing his eyes
he shuts out the sting
of too faithful memory.
Of fumes
from a smoke grenade
marking the landing zone.
Of team members
on board waiting,
wiping baby faces
with green sleeves.

Overhead,
an exhaust fan
hums, turns, pulls
kitchen smoke snakelike,
sliding
through the ceiling.

One hand
on counter top,
another
on starboard railing,
He leans into the night.
Propeller blades slice
the dark in-between.

"We're here LT."

He watches his hands.
One belongs to
someone else…
somewhere else.

"You want a refill - or
not Darlin?"

Two hands push
His too full cup
across the counter,
through the mist
into Now.

He hears
Another voice
answer,
"No thanks.
I've had enough."

Mac

Welcome Home

Only the feathers floating round the hat
Showed that anything more spectacular had occurred
Than the usual drowning.
The police preferred to ignore
The confusing aspects of the case.
And the witnesses ran off to a PTA meeting.
So the report filed and forgotten in the archives simply
read, "Drowned" but it was wrong:
Icarus had swum away coming at last to a city
Where he rented a house and tended the garden

That nice Mr. Smith the neighbors call him
Never dreaming that the gray respectable suit
Concealed arms that had controlled huge wings
Nor that the sad, defeated eyes had once
Compelled the sun. And that had he told them
They would have answered with a shocked,
uncomprehending stare

No, he could not disturb their neat front yards
Yet all his books insisted this was a horrible mistake:
What was he doing in the suburb?
Can the genius of the hero fall
To the middling stature of
the merely talented?

And nightly, Mr. Smith probes his wound
And daily in his workshop, with curtains carefully
drawn
Constructs small wings and tries to fly

To the lighting fixture on the ceiling:
Fails every time and
hates himself for trying

He had thought himself a hero,
had acted heroically
But now rides in carpools
Serves on various committees
and wishes -
he had drowned

Adapted from, *Icarus*
Edward Fields, 1952

The Long Road Home

Broken home
Left alone
Fled the known
All those clones
Marine Corps
Peace Corps
Life Taker
Life Saver
Bullet holes
Broken hearts
Divine goddess
Total loss
Sahara nights
Jungle rites
Non-profits
NGOs
Bureaucrats
Same ole crap
Family man
American plan
Homeowner
Sudden loner
Faraway places
Same ole faces
Lone Ranger
Stoic stranger
Hitchhiker
Demon biker
Workshops, books
Spiritual crooks

Born again
Died again
Peyote eater
Soul seeker
Public service
Drunken menace
Activist, Catalyst
Union socialist
Ashrams
Communes
Esoteric schools
Gurus
Shamans
Charlatans
& Fools
Revelation
Incarnation
Transformation
Disintegration
Knew It All…..
Before the Fall
Lonely hiker
Pied Piper
Golden years
Fewer fears
Another cycle
Peace somehow
In this circle
Here and now

                                    Mac

Part VII
Why Expressive Writing?

Personal writing for 25-20 minutes a day produces meaningful changes both physically and mentally. It can also help with sleep, work and socializing with others. Those who feel their trauma a secret suffer far more symptoms and doctor visits over time. Participants in emotional writing classes experience documented and measureable benefits:

Biological Effects
    Enhancement of immune system function
    Better functioning during chronic illness
    Reduced stress, blood pressure and heart rate
Behavioral Changes
    Better adjustment to social situations and school
    Enhanced employability

Psychological Effects
    New and useful mood changes and reflection after writing
    Well-being increases after weeks or a few months of writing
    Lessening of depression and anxiety

Who Benefits from Writing?
    Previous education levels play no part in the value of expressive writing
    Spelling, grammar, handwriting do not matter
Culture, social class and foreign languages everyone benefits

Talk Therapy vs. Writing

We often hold back in groups or with a counselor. There are always issues of compatibility, trust, empathy and professional competence. Even the most expressive and open person can sometimes avoid or fear talking about a particular issue or experience. The purpose of expressive writing is to be completely open and honest with your Self. Your audience is you, you alone.

Forms of Expressive Writing

A documented and annotated non-fiction approach to an autobiography: a beneficial therapeutic exercise
A book length personal memoir
Short stories
Journaling
Guided exercises focusing on personal healing
Letters, Poetry, Plays, Songs, Emails, Blogs

Approach

Acknowledgement of feelings, both positive and negative is part of storytelling.

Construction a Coherent Story

A structural goal of therapeutic writing is to put broken pieces back together again... where, who, how, when, why and sequence?

The Process
Switching Perspective

Writers benefit most when adding another view

of an incident, episode, experience or trauma.
Such as seen through the eyes of a civilian,
friend or enemy.

Find Your Voice

Cold dispassionate journalism is the job of
reporters. Your written voice and feeling will
develop as you write and reflect who you are.

Writing by Hand or Typing

Do what makes you feel most comfortable. Try
both. A microphone with voice recognition
software can type for you. This capability is
frequently preloaded on all newer computers.

Potential Dangers in Writing

The sensation of losing control by reliving the
trauma*: stop, leave, breathe, and go for a walk*
Overanalyzing: Some topics are as
understandable as they will ever be in the
rational mind.
Someone may read your journal or diary
without permission: take precautions
Life changes through Self discovery: if
confusing see, your counselor, seek out a
confidant or put the manuscript down
and take a break. Is the change desirable?
Deal only with known trauma: avoid false
memories, speculation
Let sleeping dogs lie: some issues need to be
put to rest and you will intuitively recognize
these moments.

Remember

Trust where writing takes you: a part of You- is leading the way.

Writing Instructions

For this first week after class, commit to writing on your own, at least 20 minutes a day. As this is a therapeutic writing class, suggested topics are:
A recent traumatic episode
An ongoing emotional upheaval
Chronic injury, illness, divorce, abuse, intrusive thoughts, etc.
Trauma in the past
War, abuse, injustice, etc.
Trauma in the future
Death in the family, career, finances, etc.

When and Where to Write

Create a special environment; coffee house, park, library, den, attic, etc.
Create a ritual; first exercise or meditate, shower, eat, etc.
Use the same time and comfortable writing materials each time
Write continuously: no stopping for grammar, spelling= just go!
If you get stuck, rewrite what you have just written. It will come.
Write only for your Self, your eyes only, no sharing is expected. This is a journey.
When ready, share your story.

GETTING STARTED

Read these prompts. Immediately begin writing one sentence! Go quickly on to the next phrase until you finish the page. If you go blank, skip on to the next. Should anxiety develop, get up and come back after enough time has passed to cool off.

The one thing I'll never write about is...

Maybe if....

I have lost myself since...

Does it ever seem like...

When you least expect it...

If only we...

Only thing missing was...

Don't worry I won't...

I wonder what it would take...

What I really want to know is...

What if...

It's not what you think, it's...
The truth is...

Only thing I know for sure is…

All I ever wanted was…

These days I find myself…

Things were different when…

The best part of my tour was…

Write three or four sentences. Express whatever enters your mind and don't worry about grammar, spelling or 'making sense'. Many guided journals and manuals are available for expansion on Amazon.

Suggested Topics for Your Weekly Journal
How have I changed?
How has my partner changed and things between us?
Changes with family friends, neighbors?
How have my goals and career changed?
What have I gained most or missed out on as a   result of deployment?
How did my friends and family see/describe me before deployment?
How did my friends and family see/describe me when I returned from deployment?
How do my friends and family see/describe me now?
How would you like to see myself in a few years from now?

Get the Sunday Paper. Pull out the Obituaries
Read. Write you own
How do you want to be remembered?

Name_____

Age_____

Born and Raised Where?

_____

_____

Education, Employment, Military

_____

_____

Accomplishments, Organizations, Veteran History,
Groups, Volunteer Affiliation, Travels, Hobbies,
Favorite Experiences, Regrets, Fondest Memories

_____

_____

_____

_____

Qualities of Character

_____

_____

_____

Church, Religion, View of Life

_____

_____

Names of Parents Spouse, Siblings, Children, Grandchildren_____

_____

_____

Suggested Readings

There are many anthologies, memoirs and collections of short stories by veterans from every war. One of the most respected in the last few years is: *Veterans of War, Veterans of Peace,* edited by Maxine Hong Kingston.

Perhaps the greatest examination of a nation at war and the literature of its warriors is found in Pull Fussell's, *The Great War and Modern Memory.* You will find the timeless nature of the battlefield experience and the lifelong attempt of combatants to express the inexpressible.

An entire syllabus for a semester class with selected readings can be downloaded for free: Operation Homecoming: Writing the Wartime Experience.

www.nea.gov/national/homecoming/guide.html

It's your turn now. It's time to tell your story. If you get stuck, contact me at:

brentonmack@yahoo.com

The Legacy Project

Founded in 2006, the Legacy Project is an independent endeavor to better understand how humans can transition from violent, bloody conflict to peace, justice, and reconciliation. At the center of our work are annual study trips to countries struggling to resolve their own legacies of violence, including Poland in 2007, South Africa in 2008, and Chile and Argentina in 2009.

"We believe personal messages offer unique insight into warfare and the thoughts and perspectives of those who have experienced it firsthand. Wartime letters and e-mails are also powerful reminders that U.S. troops are not just soldiers, sailors, airmen, Marines, and Coast Guardsmen; they are husbands and wives, brothers and sisters, sons and daughters, fathers and mothers. Every one of these individuals has a distinct voice and personality, and our mission is to preserve their stories, expressed in their own words."

Topics may include, but are not limited to:
    Thoughts on leaving home
    Basic training (and boot camp) experiences
    Descriptions of combat
    Love letters
    Descriptions of what it's like to be wounded in
        action
    Descriptions of heroic acts performed by fellow
        servicemen and women
    Letters by prisoners of war

Letters written in code

Descriptions of historic events

Encounters with prominent military leaders

Humorous letters ("gripes" and funny anecdotes)

Letters of advice to children or younger siblings
   back home

"Dear John" rejection letters

Letters from the home front describing life and
   current events in the United States

"Last" letters written by servicemen or women
   before they were killed in action

Reflections on war (including letters by pacifists
   and war protestors)

Letters written to or in memory of fallen comrades

Letters written by different generations of troops
   from the same family.

Letters by veterans written months, years, or even
   decades after their service that offer
   observations or opinions that could not be (or
   were not) expressed during wartime.
   Letters by service members from other nations
   Above all, any letter (or e-mail) that describes
   an incredible story or articulates thoughtfully
   the nature of war and its profound effect on
   those involved.

Established Writing Programs
For Veterans

The Hospitalized Veterans Writing Project: the mission of which is "to encourage veterans to write, through the coordinated efforts of volunteers and/or VA medical center staff. Veterans often experience traumatic and life-changing experiences in the service of their country. Writing serves as therapy for many veterans who participate through VA medical centers." www.veteransvoices.org/mission

The National Endowment for the Arts' Operation Homecoming: brings "the transformative power of writing to men and women who have undergone enormously challenging experiences in Iraq and Afghanistan. In historical terms, it gives voice to the troops who have served in this war." "Since 2004, the NEA Operation Homecoming writing program has collected the stories of U.S. military personnel and their families. With support from The Boeing Company, Operation Homecoming has brought more than 60 writing workshops to troops at more than 30 domestic and overseas military installations from Camp Pendleton in California to USS Carl Vinson in the Persian Gulf and Bagram Airfield in Afghanistan." www.arts.endow.gov/national/homecoming/index.html

VetArt Project – "creates opportunities for veterans and their family members to work in collaboration with artists from all disciplines to create new art about war for public performance and viewing.

Our goals are to support our veterans, create stronger voices among our veterans, provide new opportunities for artists, and offer a venue to hear the voices of our veterans and artists, and foster discussions about how war affects us all." vetartproject.com/

Warrior Writers – "creates a culture that articulates veterans' experiences and provides the opportunity for a creative community for artistic expression among veterans. We provide witness to the lived experiences of warriors. Through writing/artistic workshops that are based on their experiences in the military, Afghanistan and Iraq, participants connect with other veterans on a personal and artistic level. Art is compiled into books, performances and exhibits that provide a lens into the hearts of people who experienced war. www.warriorwriters.org/

The Iraq Veterans Writing Workshop: a free, non-partisan outreach program offered by the New York University Writing Program to the veterans' community in and around New York City. contact person: zachary.sussman@nyu.edu

VetsWrite4Life – "Veterans of war, ANY war, or veterans of the wounds of living, particularly if you are suffering from PTSD, join with a community of people who are writing their way back from shame. We're following method developed by Maxine Hong Kingston in her ongoing veterans writing workshops. Tell your story as it happened or in fiction. Prose, poetry or whatever is OK as long as it's honest. You can request feedback or not. You can ask for comments or critiques about a specific aspect of your writing that will make it clearer and stronger." groups.yahoo.com/group/VetsWrite4Life/

Vet's Midwest Writing Workshop: midwestvetswritingworkshop.com

Many other colleges, universities and adult ed schools also offer writing workshops and classes specifically for veterans, who are attending classes after deployment. If you are interested in exploring a local writing program, contact your county VA service representative and the web sites of your regional schools.

AND LAST...

Just What Does the VA Do Well?

The Hard Hats!

In the late 1970's, the Office of Data Management and Telecommunications (ODM&T) was given the job to computerize the VA nationwide [Brown, SH,2003]. It was developed using Massachusetts General Hospital Utility Multi-Programming System (MUMPS), or alternatively, M programming language.

In 1977, the Department of Medicine & Surgery, the predecessor of VHA, created the Computer-Assisted System Staff (CASS) Office. They involved clinical experts in the process of computerization of the medical centers, and avoided the lengthy traditional administrative process used by ODM&T. Their Decentralized Hospital Computer Program (DHCP) included programs for administration, mental health, radiology and dietetics. They also focused on re-usability and the adherence to an active data dictionary, two characteristics that were declared in a conference in December 1982.

The ODM&T tried to shut down development, but DHCP developers continued their work. DHCP developers referred to themselves as the "Hard Hats" and worked secretly on DHCP against direct orders from ODM&T. One of the reasons for the success of DHCP was that its robust infrastructure enabled individuals to develop independent applications.

This allowed developers to work on DHCP applications separately while they waited for approval to put their modules together into a cohesive system. Eventually VA Administrator Robert Nimmo approved a policy giving facility directors the power to choose computer applications in 1982. A first group of 25 sites and 11 applications was in place by 1983. These were followed by up to 100 sites in year 1985.

In 1995, DHCP was enshrined as a recipient of the Computerworld Smithsonian Award for best use of Information Technology in Medicine. A year later, the name VistA was officially given to the much improved system after the addition of a visual layer written using Delphi.

By 1999, multimedia online patient records were provided in VistA. Images from specialties such as cardiology, pulmonary and gastrointestinal medicine, pathology, radiology, hematology and nuclear medicine were supported.

As of 2001, it was the largest system in use in the US, with medical documentation and ordering available at every VA hospital in the country. In September 2002, 90.6% of all inpatient and outpatient pharmacy orders were entered by the provider. Today, the system is in use in hundreds of hospitals and clinics worldwide, not just in the VA Hospital System.

By 2003, the VHA was the largest single medical system in the United States, providing care to over 4 million veterans, employing 180,000 medical personnel and operating 163 hospitals, over 800 clinics, and 135 nursing homes. About a quarter of the nation's population is potentially eligible for VA benefits and services because they are veterans, family members, or survivors of veterans. By providing electronic health records capability, VistA is thereby one of the most widely used EHRs in the world. Nearly half of all US hospitals that have a full implementation of an EMR are VA hospitals using VistA.

As of 2009, VISTA incorporates all of the benefits of DHCP as well as including the rich array of other information resources that are becoming vital to the day-to-day operations at VA medical facilities. It represents the culmination of DHCP's evolution and metamorphosis into a new, open system, client-server based environment that takes full advantage of commercial solutions, including those provided by Internet technologies.

There are approximately 140 Department of Veterans Affairs (VA) databases in use across the country in VA facilities that are accessible via VistA systems.

The ability to uniquely identify a patient and the facilities where that patient receives care is a key factor in the delivery of quality care. The ability to uniquely identify patients assists in the elimination of duplicate records throughout all VA systems and other agencies, and allows the systems to share information for patients that receive care from more than one facility/agency.

Also by the Author...

Winning the War Within:
PTSD and the Long Road Home

This is the true story of an ordinary American caught up in the stormy decade of the 1960s. We meet him as he fails to avoid the draft, stumbles into the Marine Corps and finds Shangri La in the midst of chaos and destruction in Vietnam. Changed forever and unable to reenter his own community, the reader journeys with the veteran as he seeks to understand personal transformation through serving others as they navigate their own challenges with Post Traumatic stress Syndrome.

Grandpa, What Did You Do
On the Way to the Rest Home?

Ever wonder what happened to that kid who always got you into trouble? He's back! Admit it, you've missed him...

You are invited to join a childhood friend from down the old block and fasten your seatbelt for a roller coaster ride with no tracks. This collection of true episodes from an unplanned life will make you glad you chose to stay at home or cause you pack your bag and leave the safety of the known world before it's too late! So come on along...

About the Author

A wounded and decorated Marine in Vietnam, Brent MacKinnon worked in a dozen foreign countries and in the U.S. with refugees and Native Americans, He developed social service programs, taught language and culture from elementary school to the university level and also served twice in the Peace Corps.

Brent now lives in Northern California where he writes, teaches, travels and participates in Lego construction projects with grandson, Chase. Presently he continues to interview with organizations and agencies in the search of a mentoring program that matches older and younger vets. It's a bit challenging for two reasons.

Most young vets do not relate to the older generation (even though we have been just as screwed up and for much longer) and while staff have good intentions they often trail along behind them a baggage train of self validating therapeutic modules, the need for dissertation data, over analyzed pie charts and the need to lubricate funding streams by creatively reporting those twin demons: positive statistics and measureable results. Iraq and Afghanistan vets will need an ole timer or to refer to their own 'chat rooms' as they navigate the minefield of the VA bureaucracy.

Perhaps this new generation of vets will embrace the leadership skills acquired in the military and develop relevant and efficient self-help and advocacy programs. Who knows better?

CPSIA information can be obtained
at www.ICGtesting.com
Printed in the USA
LVHW081815231219
641488LV00037B/1843/P